THE D-I-Y GUIDE TO
Natural Stonework

J. A. C. Harrison

*With line illustrations by the author and
photographs by Jack Cooper*

DAVID & CHARLES
Newton Abbot   London   North Pomfret (Vt)

British Library Cataloguing in Publication Data
Harrison, J A C
 The D-I-Y guide to natural stonework.
 1. Building, Stone – Amateurs' manuals
 693.1   TH1201

 ISBN 0–7153–7840–6

Library of Congress Catalog Card Number: 79–52987

Typeset by
Northern Phototypesetting Co., Bolton
and printed in Great Britain
by Redwood Burn Limited, Trowbridge & Esher
for David & Charles (Publishers) Limited
Brunel House, Newton Abbot, Devon

Published in the United States of America
by David & Charles Inc.
North Pomfret, Vermont 05053 USA

Contents

Introduction

It is a sad fact that the traditional craftsman builder is almost a character of the past. The completion of Liverpool Cathedral appears to have been the work of a last generation of stonemasons. To those who may be left I apologise for the oversimplifications in this book. If it appears that I have given scant treatment to their craft, they, more than anyone, must realise that it is not a craft easily learnt from the printed word, and I hope they will find some small consolation in my attempts to revive interest in, and give a basic understanding of, what is involved in working with stone.

I have used the term 'stonework' throughout the book to mean naturally occurring stone that has been altered only by cutting, polishing, or shaping. I have excluded all reference to work with artificial stone, whatever the claims of the manufacturers for the different varieties.

The other term used throughout the book is 'random' stone, that is, stone shaped in much the same way as nature produced it and therefore occurring in a wide variety of shapes and sizes. With this type of stone the stoneworker's skill is primarily involved in the interlocking of such irregular shapes while observing sound building principles.

By narrowing the book's terms of reference to random-natural stonework, it should be possible to bring to many people an understanding of, and a guide for working with, stone in the form in which it is most readily available.

Although stone is one of the commonest – and most useful – materials on our earth, it has unfortunately become one of the most neglected. Our resources of stone would more than meet all our present building needs, whereas today we rely almost entirely on artificial and inferior substitutes. Not only are most of these less strong and less attractive but, in terms of the limited resources of the earth, they are more costly to produce.

The limestones, sandstones, granites, slates, and others that can be used as building material are immensely strong – their load-bearing properties far exceed those of any artificial material, however reinforced. They are incredibly durable, too. If it were not so, the science of archaeology might never have been born. One somehow doubts that the scientists of the future will learn much from the remains of our modern housing estates! Yet the modern and the traditional *can* come together and work well. A combination of external stonework and internal blockwork provides the advantages of cavity construction, ease of interior decoration, and speed of erection, together with all the natural advantages of stone.

However, as aspiring Do-It-Yourself stoneworkers you are unlikely to contemplate anything as complicated or as large as an actual dwelling in stone, but I hope to help you to add some interesting and attractive features to your home and garden – stonework, if you like, to live *with*, rather than live *in*!

1 Tools and Equipment

Choice of Tools

The basic tool requirements of the DIY stoneworker are few compared with those of the carpenter, and readily find other uses in the home and garden. It is essential to buy well, however, avoiding both expensive gimmicks and cheap 'bargains'. With care, the purchases, like the work for which they are designed, should last a lifetime – at least! A fairly comprehensive list of tools is given below, but not all are essential for modest constructions; those that are will be indicated.

Specialist equipment is also available that can reduce the amount of labour needed and sometimes enhance the appearance of the work. Generally, though, it would be better for the DIY person to hire rather than buy this equipment. It is worthwhile remembering that very beautiful monuments were produced long before such aids were invented, and that the knowledge and skill of the person using any tool remains of paramount importance.

Trowels

Of all the stoneworker's tools, the most essential and versatile, and yet the most often ill-chosen and abused, is the trowel. Only one trowel is required and it will quickly become an extension of your arm, instantly recognisable by feel, not appearance. It is used for more than transferring cement mortar from barrow to wall. It is seldom put down, and is used to tap stones into place, to clean old mortar from reclaimed stone, to chip off a jutting projection of rock, or even to split a batten. It is designed for one function but, chosen well, serves many. Generally termed a *builder's trowel* (Fig 1a), the blade should be approximately 27cm (10–11in) long, and approximately 15cm (6in) at the shoulders. Initially, this may appear very large to the inexperienced hand but it can do all that smaller trowels do, and much that they cannot.

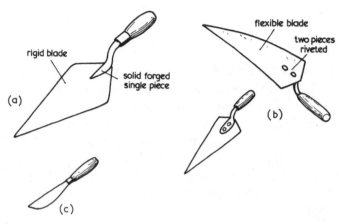

Fig 1 (a) Builder's trowel (b) trowels to avoid (c) pointing tool

The blade itself must be fairly rigid, bending only slightly under pressure – a trowel with the flexibility of a palette knife has severe limitations. The handle should also be inspected carefully. I prefer wood because it seems to adapt itself quickly to the individual grip and does not produce blisters; other stoneworkers favour the new composite handles. Whatever the personal choice, select the trowel for its feel in the hand: the small-handed person will experience unimaginable torments after gripping a handle with a very large diameter for any length of time. It is also essential to ensure that the tang is driven very firmly into the socket of the handle as any looseness there is quickly aggravated and rapidly produces a 'swivelling trowel' and a frayed temper. Finally, the join of the handle to the blade should be inspected and tested for strength by bending it back. Be particularly suspicious where the join is made by a couple of rivets (Fig 1b). Many an apparently good bargain has quickly become two worthless pieces of metal because of a basic weakness here. The best trowels are forged from a single piece of metal, shaped to give both the tang and the blade.

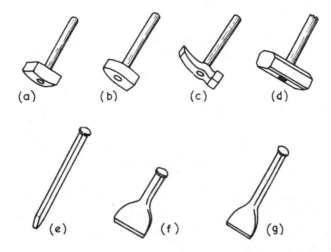

Fig 2 (a) Club or lump hammer (b) mason's hammer (c) small mason's or bricklayer's hammer (d) sledgehammer (e) cold chisel (f) bolster chisel (g) mason's or pitching chisel

Hammers

Several types of hammer are shown in Fig 2, but perhaps the most useful and, nowadays, the most easily obtained is the club or lump hammer. Here the weight of the hammer is very important, the ideal weight being about 1kg (2lb) – slightly lighter than that favoured by most manufacturers. When using a hammer and chisel all day long, the difference of half a kilo is often the difference between completing the job with ease and failing to complete it without accident. The hitting power of hammers around this weight is not generally very important; the ability to strike accurately and with minimum effort *is*.

The type of handle selected is a matter of personal choice. A number of foreign hammers are available with hollow composite handles that reduce the overall weight and the amount of shock transmitted to the hand. Most British hammers, on the other hand, still have traditional wooden handles. Because the club-hammer handle is often used to tamp down stones, particularly when paving, wooden handles split and curl at the end. So, if tempted to use it in this way, buy the hammer with the composite-material handle.

The small mason's or bricklayer's hammer, is particularly

useful when paving, where the chisel end can be used to shape and split the slabs. It is good for walling, too, for knocking stubborn projections off stones, and so on. As it is generally too light to be used with a cold chisel – the small surface area of the head often results in skids, misses, and bruised fingers – where there is a choice to be made between it and a lump hammer the lump hammer should be selected. The modern mason's hammer, apart from being very difficult to obtain, combines the functions of the lump hammer on one striking surface with a splitting and shaping tool on the other. Its use requires some considerable skill and knowledge of the properties of the stone being worked, and so is not initially recommended for the DIY stoneworker's toolbox.

Sledgehammers are mainly used for breaking up large chunks of rock. They are available in a great variety of weights, but one of around 3·5kg (7lb) should suit most purposes without demanding Herculean strength. With all wooden-handled striking tools – and particularly sledgehammers – the grain in the handle should be carefully examined. Ideally, this should run straight and even for the length of the shaft. Where the grain runs out of the handle a splitting weakness occurs, and any shaft showing a very short grain length, or irregularities near the head, should be rejected. A sledge-hammer version of the mason's hammer is also available.

Chisels

A wide and bewildering array of different chisels (Fig 2e, f, g) is available for working with stone. Many are for specialised decorative work and do not concern us here. Unfortunately, there is no single multi-purpose chisel for stonework, so the DIY enthusiast will probably require three or four chisels to be able to tackle most types of jobs.

The bolster chisel is the basic splitting tool, indispensable for splitting regularly grained rocks for paving and cladding. The wide slim blade transmits the energy of the hammer blow along the seam, rather than concentrating it at a single point. There is little to choose between various bolsters: some are available with rubber protective rings to soften the blow from an ill-aimed hammer, and there are slight differences in the size and the thickness of the blades.

Cold chisels are used, and perhaps legitimately abused, for a wide range of tasks and, like a many-bladed scout's knife, are called upon to prise the lid off a stubborn can one moment, and act as a makeshift plumb bob the next. They are mainly used for cutting out old mortar, for repointing work, for cutting out defined areas of concrete or mortar, for roughly shaping stone and paving and, as a general prising and loosening tool, for demolition work. Two cold chisels of differing size are probably sufficient: one large, approximately 25–30cm (10–12in) long, with a cutting width of about 2·5cm (1in) for heavy work, and a smaller chisel with a cutting width of about 1·25cm (½in) for delicate work, particularly where old stonework needs to be renovated.

The pitching chisel – also termed a *pitching tool* or *mason's chisel* – is something of a cross between the cold chisel and the bolster, but is not easy to obtain. It is indispensable for dressing stones and paving, but, like the mason's hammer, requires experience of stone itself to obtain the best result. It is worth purchasing by the DIY person, and should be experimented with to get the feel of the tool and compare it with the bolster and cold chisel. But since we are mainly concerned with random stonework, it need not be regarded as essential, for many of its functions can be carried out with either the bolster or the cold chisel.

Pointing tools

A pointing tool (Fig 1c) is essential for cutting out the mortar joints, pointing up, and generally cleaning the stonework. Unfortunately, such a tool is not manufactured and, after using various implements, from kitchen knife to trowel, I have found by far the best substitute to be a putty knife. This should be slightly more flexible than the trowel, but not too much so, and can be partially modified on a grindstone to produce the most suitable shape for the type of joint finish required (*See* Chapter 3, Pointing). As this is also the most frequently misplaced item in the tool-kit, a good coat of bright paint on the handle saves a considerable amount of time spent looking for it.

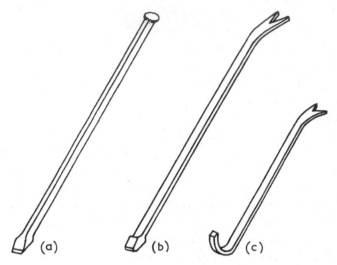

Fig 3 (a) The basic multipurpose bar (b) and (c) specialist bars to avoid

Bars

The different types of bar (Fig 3) available almost rival the array of chisels but only one type is essential to the stoneworker. Ideally, this should be straight and between 1·5m and 2m (5–6ft) in length, and of sturdy diameter, yet not too large to suit the hand. Only one end should be pointed to a chisel shape, the other flattened so that it may be struck by the sledge. This bar is the basic levering tool of the stoneworker, whether in demolition, quarrying, or simply moving and positioning large stones. It is also extremely effective for splitting large rocks where there is a distinctive grain, and as a solid marking pole for large constructions. The simplicity of the straight bar provides a versatility of uses that far outweighs any advantages to be gained from purchasing special bars for specific tasks.

Shovels

Many makes of shovels are advertised and, apart from a few basic considerations, the final choice of design will be one of personal preference. Avoid light alloy shovels and the extra large shovels favoured by stevedores and farmers. On grounds of durability, the all-metal labourer's shovel is better than the wooden-handled type. Also, you will find the D-handle to have advantages over the T-shape. Again, it is more durable, easier to swing, and less likely to cause blisters, but there are others who swear by the T-shape. Perhaps the best advice is to continue to use the shape with which you are already familiar and find most comfortable.

Levels and bobs

A spirit level (Fig 4) is essential to the stoneworker. Chosen well, the spirit level can perform several functions other than its intended one. It can provide a good 'straight-edge', can be marked off as a rule to give accurate basic measurements, and can double as a plumb bob for checking the vertical face of a wall or 'return' – the change in direction of a wall.

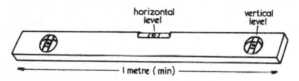

Fig 4 A spirit level

The spirit level should be no less than 1m (3¼ft) and probably no more than 1·25m (4ft) in length. The bubbles should be adjustable, changeable, and visible from more than one direction. The accuracy of the horizontal and the vertical bubbles can be checked against a window – builders are particularly careful about windows, where any slight irregularities are immediately apparent – and speedily corrected with the turn of a screw or, if damaged, replaced. The choice of wood or metal is again personal, and probably makes little difference if the other conditions are satisfied. Where a level needs to be checked or determined over greater distances or across circular constructions, a good length of straight planed timber – about 3m (10ft) long – is most useful and can be handled in conjunction with the level. If painted white and marked out, the timber can double as a quick and convenient measuring rod.

The plumb bob is designed for gauging the accuracy of the

perpendicular (vertical) face or end of a wall. Unfortunately, when working outside in a wind it can give rise to exasperating gyrations! As an alternative, use a spirit level or a batten plumbed and fixed into place. It is more convenient and stable. Should a plumb-line be necessary, a loop of string around a cold chisel or an old fishing-weight will suffice.

Line levels may also be purchased, but they are not really an essential part of the DIY tool-kit. They are meant to slide along the plumb-line to ensure that it is level – particularly important at the 'topping-off' stage – but the level itself always seems to depress the line, however taut. The spirit level and batten can perform the same function without this drawback.

Line and line pins

A good line is indispensable. 'Making do' with odds and ends of string, clothes line, and so on will probably ruin any project. Fine nylon builders' line can be purchased in varying lengths, usually up to about 50m (165ft) but, although favoured by bricklayers, it does not last very long. It often gets cut – particularly when digging out foundations and footings or when topping-off – by an ill-aimed blow from shovel or trowel. It also seems to camouflage itself amongst the stone and tends to be forgotten or to become so mortar-encrusted that it is finally abandoned.

A satisfactory line material is, in fact, an agricultural product which, though expensive, has many advantages and can be obtained in kilometre, rather than metre, lengths. It is of a woven, bright orange polypropylene material with a fine wire plaited through it. (Its normal use is usually as temporary electrical fencing.) The line is little thicker than old-fashioned fibre string and is extremely tough and easily cleaned. Although it stretches a little initially, when tightened the stretching quickly ceases and a taut line can be achieved over considerable distances between two firmly fixed poles. For the same reason that it resists accidental chopping and breakage well, it is also troublesome to cut into the desired lengths.

Line pins are not always required by stoneworkers who, unlike bricklayers, do not build in a continuous succession of level courses. In certain circumstances, however, they are very handy, and an investment in a couple of good pins, in non-rusting metal, is worthwhile.

Picks and 'grubbers'

Picks, or pickaxes, and grubbers are the basic hacking and groundwork tools of the stoneworker and, of the two, the pick is the more useful. The grubber is similar in construction to the pick – and indeed the handles are interchangeable – but one of the blades on the head of the former is of an elongated hoe shape. The grubber, in point of fact, is really a gardening tool designed for cutting through roots, digging out scrub, and breaking up stony compacted ground; it is probably too light for the work demanded from the pick. This, apart from its digging functions, serves to prise and lever stubborn or large stones out of place and is useful in demolition work. It is also indispensable for levering up old floors and paths and is necessary for tamping new paving into place. Most heads are of similar weight and style. Avoid extremes of size, and make sure that the handles are sturdy, since the leverage that can be applied with a carefully placed pick is phenomenal.

Brooms and brushes

Unfortunately, there is not any one type of broom or brush that will handle all the jobs the stoneworker requires of it. For general cleaning-up, a large stiff-handled yard broom is necessary; for grouting, paving, and removing fine dust, a soft bristle is essential. Nowadays, brooms with artificial fibres are probably the best buys and, as always, test them out a bit in the shop to satisfy yourself that the bristles are firmly fixed, the handles don't snap like matchsticks, and that the heads do not fall off after a slight bump.

Hand brushes are less often used, but a good wire brush is very useful for cleaning the splashes or bits of mortar that tend to accumulate on any construction, and it is indispensable for removing old lime, plaster dust, or whitewash during renovation work. It also comes in handy for buffing up the trowel you forgot to clean properly after you last used it!

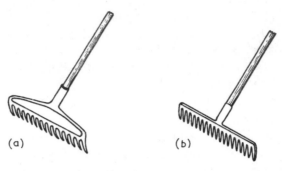

Fig 5 Rakes; type (a) is more useful for obtaining good levels than type (b)

Rakes

For any paving or flooring work a good rake (Fig 5) can save many hours of toil. It is the ideal tool for spreading and levelling loose material, such as soil and gravel, and, with a little skill, even mortar and concrete. It is a pity that many people are unaware that the back of the rake can be used as often as the teeth and, for that reason, type (a) illustrated is preferable. Also, as rake handles rarely outlive their heads buy from those manufacturers offering shaped, replaceable, handles to fit their tools.

Buckets and drums

Buckets used for carrying water and mixing additives for the mortars quickly become stained and thus are of little other use. The old-fashioned metal buckets – whilst admittedly hardy – become dented and misshapen, and are prone to both rusting and becoming encrusted with cement. Light plastic buckets, on the other hand, seem either to split or shatter or lose their handles within a few hours of hard use. Only the really heavy duty polyethylene buckets stand up to the sort of treatment that buckets are given in building work. They have to cope not only with liquid contents but also with transporting rubble and mortar to those awkward areas that barrows cannot reach. Like the lines, these buckets are obtainable from agricultural suppliers and this in itself is a recommendation for durability. They are now increasingly common in hardware and DIY stores.

When mixing quantities of mortar – and stonework requires more than most other forms of material – the constant journey to and from the tap for water becomes a chore. The most effective solution is a drum or a water-storage vessel that can be located beside the mixing area and filled with a hose. When water is required, the bucket is simply dipped into it – and it is available for washing your tools at the end of the day. The 40-gallon ex-oil drum is the ubiquitous container of the construction industry but can hardly be recommended as a beautiful addition to the garden. A new galvanised dustbin or a polyethylene water butt, however, would not be out of place and would find other uses when the building work has been completed. These have a further advantage: they are provided with lids or covers. Water and large containers seem to have a fascination for small children. If they should fall head first into a drum, they cannot possibly get out. Fatal accidents have occurred and unfortunately will continue to occur in water butts. Protect young children by covering the drum with a lid or by tipping out the water and leaving the drum on its side whenever you finish working.

The need for a hosepipe to fill the drum is obvious, but the hose is useful also for washing down external walling prior to repointing, and for general cleaning tasks. Once again, spend your money wisely and purchase an adequate length – at least the total length of the garden – of good-quality hose.

Tapes and rules

Accurate measurement is unavoidable in the long run, and a good tape must be on your list of initial purchases. I prefer cloth to metal for many reasons, particularly since the now improved materials have greatly reduced stretching. Cloth does not damage easily when the odd stone or implement is accidentally dropped on the tape; it is clearer to read; and it can be purchased with metric and imperial measurements on opposite sides. We shall be using both notations in this country for many years yet, and this should be borne in mind when purchasing. A long tape can measure short and long distances with equal ease; a short one cannot; so purchase a tape not less than 30m (100ft) long. Finally, as spring-loaded rewinds tend to weaken with usage, opt for a manual rewind handle.

Rigid measuring rules are not essential for DIY stonework. In the section on levels I have already mentioned the DIY multi-purpose batten that can perform this function.

Protective gear

For certain types of work some form of protective clothing is a sensible precaution. Prolonged periods of handling unfamiliar tools soon give rise to blisters; cement and old lime and mortars dry out the skin and cause cracking sores – or even dermatitis – in just a single day. So use gloves to protect your hands. Many kinds are available and for those who, like myself, abhor working in gloves, the cheap, light, cotton industrial gloves, sold in most hardware and gardening stores, offer reasonable freedom and wear quite well.

If you are going to dress stone or clean out old mortar or concrete with a hammer and chisel, I would recommend a cheap pair of industrial safety goggles. Apart from the danger of real damage from a flying chip of stone, protection from the painfully irritating mortar particles when working at head-height or above is comforting. Similarly, when brushing down an old wall, demolishing old stonework and flooring or using abrasive cutting and grinding discs, a face mask is a sensible precaution against lung irritation (or even permanent damage). Simple nose-and-mouth filter pads can be obtained very cheaply, and once you have seen the amount of rubbish that accumulates on them if working in a confined space, you will wonder why you ever worked without one before.

Feet are vulnerable to falling stones, particularly when laying paving, and anybody who insists on wearing soft canvas shoes or open sandals deserves the resulting pain. Wear good stout boots, preferably with protective toecaps. These are incorporated into a variety of footwear, including Wellingtons.

Miscellaneous

Certain other items may come in handy, but on the whole these need not be purchased, because they can be made up or cannibalised from other bits and pieces when the need arises. Battens and poles are always useful for making up framework, angles, and so on. Heavier lengths of timber are excellent for use as levers and supports. Old scaffolding boards are an excellent find. They can serve as ramps for wheelbarrows and as shuttering boards, as well as performing their particular function.

A flat mixing board known as a 'spot board', about 1 metre square (3ft sq) is also very useful. The mix can be emptied out on to it right beside the working area without staining the floor surface, and it can be raised on blocks to a comfortable working height.

Larger Equipment

With the exception of the barrow, there is little need to purchase any of the equipment listed below unless a really large project is to be undertaken. Equipment hire, if approached sensibly, can be very cheap. Don't order any machine until you need to use it; use it when you have it; don't let it stand around idle; and, when you've finished, return it. Apart from capital cost, hire has another advantage – the machine should be in well maintained order; also, any breakdowns and repairs are the responsibility of the hire firm. If you use hired tools efficiently, you will use them often and get good value for money.

Wheelbarrows

The wheelbarrow you choose must satisfy several very rigid conditions. If it does not, it is not worth considering. A barrow must carry heavy loads of up to 125kg (2½cwt) – I have, incidentally, seen four times this amount moved in a barrow – and yet be well balanced and manoeuvrable when loaded. It must be able to carry chunks of angular rock, building stone, flagstone and the like, that are more often thrown than reverently lowered into it, without crushing like an eggshell. It must be capable of transporting such a load without the wheel buckling or sinking into the ground to its axle; without the barrow remaining rock firm and only the handles lifting; without pitching and yawing like a dinghy in stormy sea; and without forcing you to bang your knees against it at every step.

It has to cope with being driven at speed up a scaffolding plank at an angle approaching 45°, and negotiate a flight of steps that would give many people vertigo. Apart from all this, it must be capable of shrugging off all the missiles (and abuse) hurled at it, and provide efficient, undemanding, and long-lasting service.

In my view, there are only two types of barrow that satisfy all these conditions and they do not seem to be at hardware or DIY stores. Firstly, there is the builders' or navvies' barrow used and well-tested over many years on all construction sites. It is supplied with either a solid or inflatable tyre. I consider the latter so superior in performance on uneven or soft ground that it more than compensates for any inconvenience such as inflating or mending punctures.

This barrow may seem expensive but it will give great service in the garden long after you have used all the stone you can find. It may appear heavy but its good balance enables most women to handle it with relative ease. Its dimensions allow it to pass through standard doorways or slip under the drum of a cement-mixer without problems.

The other type of barrow is the recently invented 'Ballbarrow' patented by Kirk Dyson Designs Ltd. Their new *builders'* version, which costs about the same as the conventional wheeled type, meets all these requirements *and* has further advantages still. To me it is without equal. Fully loaded, it can be rolled over the softest ground with ease; its bin will withstand greater mistreatment than any metal one; and mixes do not stick in it however long they are left. It doesn't rust; doesn't need oiling; and it is light enough to move around or transport away from home. The bin shape is particularly suitable for paving, but it will shift anything and in larger quantities than the conventional wheelbarrow. The ball needs no puncture kit to repair – a leak can be sealed by a lighter flame in a few seconds – and, if you ever manage to damage it, the bin is replaceable,

Cement-mixers

For most DIY stoneworkers, and particularly the inexperienced ones, even the hire of a cement-mixer may not be worth the cost. When you start walling, you will be slow and probably not use more than a bag or so of cement in a full day. For putting in foundations and laying paving, however, the rate and volume of the mixes required is greatly increased, and here a cement-mixer may be worthwhile. Obtain the light, electrically-operated type of mixer. You are unlikely to be far from a power source and will be saved the arduous tasks of obtaining fuel and continually starting an engine. An added bonus is that electric mixers are lighter and quieter than comparable petrol or diesel types and can be run directly off the domestic power supply.

Trestles and scaffolding

Working above chest-height causes certain problems that can affect the final quality of the work. The additional strain of lifting often results in only small stones being used, and also produces an unbalanced appearance in the finished job. It is, too, more difficult to maintain accurate levels, and leans and waves are produced. Thus, for tall constructions a working platform is required.

Where a couple of blocks and a plank may suffice for the 'odd job', work of longer duration deserves a stable, wide, and permanent platform capable of supporting the stoneworker, the materials and the tools required for the job. If adjustable trestles are hired together with good scaffolding planks, work can be comfortably carried out at up to a height of 3m (10ft); and a broad level surface is provided, even if the ground slopes. Above about 3m, stable scaffolding should be erected by a scaffolding firm. It is extremely dangerous for people unfamiliar with scaffolding to attempt such a task and, in any case, is impossible to achieve single-handed. For the DIY job, however, it is unlikely that such equipment will be needed.

Never attempt to build from a ladder! Two hands are permanently required for stonework, and often three would be more useful. More accidents result from misuse of ladders, which are simply vehicles for travelling from one stable working level to another, than from any other working aid.

Jacks

Most people regard jacks as lifting devices for vehicles, but a certain type of jack, often known by the trade name of 'Acro-jack', is also used in the building industry. This is not really a lifting device but an adjustable support indispensable where renovation work is to be carried out. Such jacks are available in various sizes, and can be used to support a series of joists where a wall has to be repaired, or support lintels over doors, windows, fireplaces, and so on, while the mortar sets.

Stone-cutters

For certain jobs, such as shaping or trimming paving stones, leaving a good edge on old concrete or tarmac where part of it has to be removed, or cutting out old blockwork, mechanical cutters are useful. If the cutters are electrically powered, they are termed *angle grinders* and generally need to be used in conjuction with a transformer when run off the domestic power supply. If petrol-driven, they run off a chain-saw type of unit. Both use an abrasive disc, and of the two I prefer the petrol version for its versatility, ease of use, and larger disc size. The discs are expensive on both machines and quickly wear out on hard stone, although they last well with the softer concrete slabs. Use them sparingly unless time is the overriding consideration.

Certain types of stone (including slate) cannot be successfully cut with a normal stone-cutter but require a water-cooled, diamond-toothed saw. In such cases, a visit to a local monumental mason would be rewarding. However, the firm Jonsereds have recently introduced a portable water-cooled stone-cutter that should greatly increase the stone-cutting scope for anyone engaged in DIY, if you can find one to hire.

Care and Usage

If this is your first venture into stoneworking, then you can see that you will have to spend a lot of money on your basic tool-kit, but I hope less than you might have done without the benefit of this book. However, even if you have already accumulated the basic kit, the next replacement will inevitably cost you more. This expense should be one reason at least for putting tools away in good order, cleaned and accounted for, at the end of the day.

Looking after your tools

Cement and cement mixes seem to stick tenaciously to everything except the surfaces for which they were intended and, once established, even tiny splashes produce rock-hard abrasive spurs that rip open flesh and slash at smoothed finishes. Many additives (*See* Chapter 2, page 42) enhance and speed this irritating phenomenon. Fortunately, before a mix hardens it is water-soluble and easily removed. Thus the first rule in tool care for the stoneworker is prevention before cure. Wash your tools regularly. That does not mean just at the end of the day but whenever you stop for a break. This is particularly true when it comes to your trowel. In no time at all it will become encrusted. While the point end may be sparkling, the farther back you go the worse it will look. Do not wait for 'some other time when you've nothing better to do'; use the drum of water and wire brush immediately. Do the same with the shovel and pointing tool.

But it is not only the tools used directly with the mixes that gradually accumulate a thick crusty coat. Your lump hammer and level, your measuring rod and wheelbarrow axle, will all, inevitably collect their share of mess. A level without a clean true surface, or with an invisible bubble, is totally useless; if you have to chop and bang away at it to remove the accretions at a later stage, you may cause permanent damage. If you can, look after your tools as you would your hands. Look after them and they will do what you require of them; if you abuse them, it will be your own fault when they let you down – providing you have chosen wisely in the first place.

Having stressed this policy of prevention when working with cement mixes, I am fully aware of the need to offer some cure. Few of us are perfect and it will probably not be long before your encrusted shovel and other tools remind you of the last job undertaken.

Metal tools

The two implements that most commonly suffer from neglect are the shovel and the trowel, and each must be tackled in different ways. If you accept that metals can vibrate and transmit a force in a direction other than that in which it is applied, you can probably work out the procedure for yourself with any tool. I have selected the shovel and trowel to illustrate two extremes of the scale.

Never try to clean the shovel – nor indeed any tool – by banging it repeatedly on the ground. Mortar is loosened by vibrating the metal. The shovel should be grasped firmly in one hand low down on the shaft, raised clear of the ground, then struck repeatedly on the back with a lump hammer or small mason's hammer. Initially, it may seem more convenient to rest the blade of the shovel on the ground and bang away. A couple of days later, however, when the handle falls off or the shaft starts to fold, you will hastily reconsider the idea.

The builder's trowel requires different treatment, again determined by its method of construction. Here, the main point of weakness is the join between the blade and the metal tang that fits into the handle. (Even trowels forged in a single piece have some degree of weakness at that particular spot.) Vibration energy will be concentrated at this point and weaken the joint; so when cleaning, it is important to dampen any vibration. Lay the blade on a flat surface – such as a paving slab or block – and, using the small mason's hammer, systematically pulverise or chip off the accretion, attacking both surfaces independently. When the rough cleaning is finished, a vigorous buffing with a wire brush and then a light greasing with waste oil will return your trowel to pristine condition.

The trowel and shovel are only two examples, but if you consider the construction of a piece of equipment and the cleaning principles involved, you should be able to handle any problem. For example, a wheelbarrow should be turned upside down to avoid damaging the wheel axle. Mixer-drums should be kept scrupulously clean preferably by scouring out with gravel or chippings after the initial wash. Striking the drum with the lump hammer soon produces dents that reduce the quality of the mix and provide new sites for mortar accumulation.

Wooden handles

Special problems occur with wooden handles and wooden implements. While they do not collect cement as readily as metal, when it *does* happen a different cleaning approach is needed. To bang or chop at the handle bruises and splinters the wood, making the tool less comfortable to use. If washing and rubbing will not remove the lumps, glass paper will do so without roughening the wood. Inaccurate blows often damage the wooden shafts of hammers and picks near the heads. To counter this, a tight binding of plastic insulating tape in this region will reduce the damage without interfering with the smoothness of the shaft to the hand. Similarly, binding the shaft where the grain does not run true will delay the onset of splitting.

Wood shrinks, particularly in dry weather or during storage, and, as a result, the heads of the tools loosen. This can be combated by immersing the heads in water for about twenty-four hours in order to swell the wood so that the heads fit tightly again. For persistently loosening heads, small wedges, either of hard wood or metal, should be driven into the base of the shaft prior to swelling in water. With regular use the shafts will remain smooth and shiny from the constant natural burnishing and oiling action of the hand. If the tools are used rarely, however, treatment with linseed oil will keep the wood from drying out and becoming brittle.

Rusting

Usage prevents rusting; but if tools are stored for prolonged periods in damp conditions, they will inevitably rust. Do not store all your hand tools together in a metal box, but separate them to allow a free circulation of air around each. In addition, a light greasing will give added protection. Pay particular attention to the wheelbarrow axle if the barrow is to be stored over the winter.

Identification

Many tricks are employed to prevent small tools being mislaid when working. The most successful method is to paint their handles in different colours, but you should remember that a hand painted surface may reduce the ease and comfort of handling. Use identification marks on those parts of the shafts that are least used.

Hints on using the tools

Many people purchase tools and automatically expect themselves to be expert in their usage, whereas it is the usage that produces the expertise. This brief section is simply intended to outline general points in handling tools; actual methods for specific tasks, such as cutting paving slabs, will be treated in the appropriate sections of Chapters 3 and 4.

With hired tools, the firms providing the equipment will generally offer instruction in their usage, since correct handling obviously prolongs the life of their machines. Take the advice offered, and try to have the working of an unfamiliar piece of equipment, such as a stone-cutter, demonstrated to you. Good hire firms should have the facilities to do this, and it is worth dealing with those that do so since such thoughtful service is likely to be reflected in other ways.

All hand tools should be held firmly – but not too tightly. Your grip and strength will develop gradually in this way without being forced. Unfortunately, very few of us are naturally ambidextrous but we can all learn to use two-handed tools, such as shovels, rakes and pickaxes, in both a left- and right-handed fashion, regardless of our natural tendencies. This provides relief, not only for arms and shoulders, but more importantly for the back, which quickly rebels against an unequal strain. The ability to make this change prolongs the period of sustained working and leaves you less tired at the end of the day. Single-handed tools, such as trowels and hammers, are harder to use with equal facility in either hand, and it is best to concentrate on learning to work calmly and comfortably with the hand most natural for you to use.

The most common minor injuries occur when handling

hammer and cold chisel. The chisel should be gripped high up – so that it does not waver – and pressed firmly against the surface to be cut, at an almost upright angle, so that skidding is minimised. When striking the chisel with the lump hammer, your eyes should concentrate on the chisel point and *not* on the top where the hammer lands. In this way you will use the two implements as a single functional unit rather than two separate ones.

The sledgehammer seems to hold a special fascination for both small boys and grown men. There is absolutely no reason whatever for the sledgehammer to be swung from behind the body. Much of the destructive energy comes from the weight of the head; you add to that by increasing the rate of the descent of the head on to the surface to be struck; you are simply wasting energy and losing control of the hammer if you raise it in a wide arc away from the body. The sledgehammer should be gripped firmly, high on the shaft, with one hand, and loosely near the head with the other, raised just above one shoulder and, using the power from your whole body, brought sharply downwards. The shaft slides lightly through the loosely gripping hand that provides directional control as well as increasing the rate of descent.

No written instruction can help the beginner to become efficient with the trowel which, initially, seems to be a most misconceived piece of equipment. The obvious temptation is to throw it down and use your hands instead! But by persevering with the trowel, by using too much mortar rather than too little, it will eventually feel natural in your hand and become an indispensable aid.

It is often necessary to lever objects out of position, particularly in demolition work, and some understanding of the basic principles of leverage is the most effective way of learning how to use levering tools, such as the bar, pickaxe, or wooden plank. In general, you will be applying force in one direction to move an object in the opposite direction, and to do so the bar or levering tool (Fig 3) must swivel on a firm hinge termed a *fulcrum*. The force transmitted to the object to be raised is greater the longer the distance between the force applied and the fulcrum. Therefore, the longer the bar you use the greater the leverage you can apply, remembering, of course, that the bar itself must be strong enough to transmit this force without bending or breaking. To lever out a stubborn stone, for example, slip the chisel end deeply beneath it, push a brick or block under the bar to act as a firm fulcrum as close to the stone as possible, and pull down on the bar (Fig 30a).

When levering stones or bricks out of a wall, slip the bar into an opened joint and use an adjacent stone as the fulcrum. The shape of the pick head enables the wooden shaft to function as a fulcrum, but great strain is placed on the handle. This will bend very slightly before it breaks, and this should be regarded as a warning not to apply further pressure.

The shovel is not really a digging tool and can only be effective on material previously loosened by the pick. It is also much easier to shovel off a clean flat surface than an uneven one; so ensure that materials such as stone and chippings are emptied on to such a surface, and work around the base of the pile rather than from the middle.

2 Materials

Stone

Origins of stone

Without going into long geological explanations, we can divide stone into three main groups according to the way in which it was formed. The oldest type of rock is termed *igneous* (fiery) rock because it came from the molten mass at the centre of the earth, and either cooled and solidified slowly deep down or was forced to the surface where it cooled rapidly. This type of stone is often crystalline in structure, and typical examples are lavas, granite, and basalt.

Particles eroded from these rocks were deposited in the oceans and there, together with the shells of tiny marine creatures, they settled to the bottom as a sediment. Gradually, they became pressed into a dense material under their own weight and that of the water above, eventually producing the type of rock we call *sedimentary*. Over millions of years layer upon layer was laid down, later to be raised again in mountains and ridges during the great upheavals of geological time. Such rocks are of two main types: where they are composed mainly of the calcium-containing shells of marine animals they are termed *limestones*; where they are mostly silica in the form of sand particles they are termed *sandstones*. All grades appear between these two extremes, the pure limestones, such as chalk, being very soft, the old red sandstones, very hard.

Because both igneous and sedimentary rocks were often subjected to great heat or pressure after they were formed, their structure was again changed to produce the third basic type, *metamorphic* rock. Limestone was changed to marble in this manner, the clays and shales to slate, and sandstone to quartzite.

Properties and characteristics

The ideal shape for a building unit is a cube or brick shape
with all surfaces flat and regular so that they can be easily laid
against each other. This perfect ideal is rarely produced
naturally, and the variations encountered are one source of
beauty in stonework. Some flat surfaces, however, are
necessary to produce a stable structure, even though the overall
shape of the unit need not be regular. Flat surfaces are most
readily obtained in rock that has been formed in regular layers
like sedimentary rock, and thus the bulk of quarried building
stone is provided by the limestones and sandstones. In the UK
limestone forms great parallel beds, often traversed by joints
(produced by folding and pressure) that run at right angles to
the beds. Thus the rock is naturally divided into sizeable
blocks, termed *freestones*, which can be further split into building
units. Limestone of this type stretches in a great arc from North
Yorkshire to South Wales and Dorset and gives rise to the
famous local building stones such as York, Pennant, and
Cotswold.

Metamorphic slates also retain their bedded character and
can be split like the sedimentary rock from which they were
formed. However, because they were subjected to further
pressure they are much denser (and impervious to water), and
can be divided into even thinner layers. Slates, therefore, are
much favoured as natural roofing and flooring material and
also for areas that are subjected to continual wear such as steps.
The best known slates come from North Wales, Cumbria, and
the West Country.

Igneous rock, with the exception of granite, generally makes
poor building material. The slow cooling of granite, however,
does produce regular cracks and fissures that enable it to be
quarried and subsequently sawn. Although very hard and
difficult to work, its beauty – particularly when polished – and
exceptional durability make it a desirable, if expensive,
building material.

Apart from quarried stone, material of convenient size is
found in most districts, although its shape may be very
irregular. The flints formed from silica deposits in chalk

country may be seen in traditional walls and buildings throughout Berkshire, Wiltshire, and Hampshire, where they are often used in combination with mellow brick. Conglomerates and agglomerates, formed of pebbles naturally cemented together, litter many parts of the country in convenient sizes for building. In mountainous areas, gradual erosion by rain and wind and the action of ice and frost, produce screes of shattered rock that form natural piles of building stone. In addition, the retreating glacial sheets of the Ice Ages have left abundant moraines of smoothed shaped stones of all types and sizes.

The stone for the job

Apart from classifying stone according to its origin, stoneworkers often find it more convenient to refer to stone according to the type of job for which it is intended. The DIY worker will be mainly concerned with three basic types of constructional stone and a further non-constructional miscellaneous group used for infilling.

Building stone or 'walling'

This can be any type of stone, providing it is not too soft (such as chalk) and is of manageable size. For random stonework a range of size and shape is used with little exact patterning or 'course-work' (*See* Chapter 3). The stones will generally be of a block type; that is, with all surfaces of similar size in a single stone (Fig 6a). However, whereas a cube has six equal flat faces, far more irregular shapes are used for random work. Any stone with as little as two or three flat surfaces, regardless of shape, can make an ideal building unit and, with a different technique, spherical and egg-shaped stones can produce walls of character. So long as the stone can be lifted to rest firmly on the one beneath and provide a firm base to accept another above, it can be used for building. Regular blocks are the easiest to use, but perhaps produce the least interesting finish. With experience, irregular shapes give the greatest satisfaction and scope for the imagination and builders should not dismiss such material as rubble and hardcore.

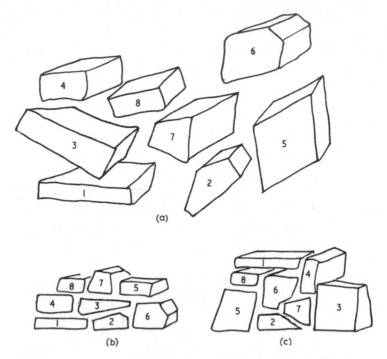

Fig 6 Building stone (a) some fairly regularly shaped blocks (b) the same blocks, laid flat – producing a small face area (c) the same, laid both flat and upright, producing a larger face area

The amount of stone required for walling work is a function of the area of each stone exposed on the finished surface of the construction. Thus, narrow flat stones laid regularly on top of each other expose only a small surface area compared to their bulk, which is hidden within the wall, and a great weight of stone is required for each square metre of the finished job (Fig 6b). Conversely, less weight per finished unit area is needed where the largest faces are exposed (Fig 6c). Some tables of quantities for building stone are provided in the Appendix but can only be used as a rough guide. Not only shape and building technique affect the weight/area relationship of walling stone, but also different types of stone vary considerably in density. Furthermore, methods of loading and transporting can affect the quality of the material delivered, and thus the proportion that is usable.

Plate 1 An example of fairly good stonework

Plate 2 An example of bad stonework

Plate 3 Slate boat-motif in a
limestone wall

Plate 4 An old stone cottage,
renovated and extended

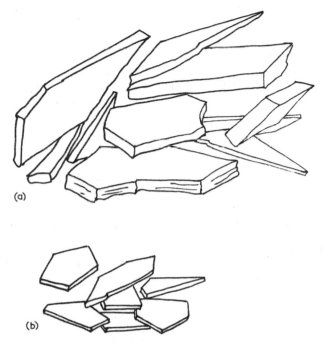

Fig 7 (a) Paving – large irregular sheets of variable thickness (b) cladding – smaller, more regular sheets of even thickness

Paving

Paving stone (Fig 7a) is more rigidly defined than walling because of the limitations placed upon it by its intended function. Paving is derived from thin sheets of sedimentary or metamorphic rock with one very smooth large surface. It can vary from about 2cm ($\frac{3}{4}$in) in thickness up to 10cm (4in). Generally, the sandstones and limestones need to be at the thicker end of the scale, because they are more friable than the harder slates. If the sheets of stone used are variable in size and outline, they produce the random effect sometimes called 'crazy paving'. Where they are cut into more formal rectangular shapes, as seen in old pavements, they are termed *flagstones*. These, when broken, can also be laid to produce a random effect. Sometimes limestone naturally occurs in sheets from 1–3cm ($\frac{3}{8}$–1$\frac{1}{8}$in) thick, often richly coloured by the seepage of water containing dissolved metal salts, mainly iron. These sheets are easy to split from the mother rock and are termed *rivings*. They provide excellent material for paving stone and also for cladding (see below) and, unlike slates, are easy to cut and shape. (Table I in the Appendix gives quantities for different thicknesses of paving.)

Cladding

'Cladding' (Fig 7b), meaning to clothe, is the technique of covering a basic structure with a decorative finish that has no structural function. Stone for cladding in building is similar to paving, but much thinner, usually only 1cm ($\frac{3}{8}$in) thick. The most commonly used natural cladding material is slate, which can be easily split into uniform thicknesses. Limestone rivings, however, can also be used when they are naturally available in such thin sheets. The necessary quantities are given in Table I of the Appendix.

Obtaining stone

Obtaining the basic material of stonework probably presents the greatest problem of all, and the telephone directory is often of little assistance. It is quite normal to suppose that natural building stone can be obtained from an operating quarry, but this is rarely the case. Most quarries nowadays seem to function solely to pulverise and grind good-quality building stone into tiny chippings and dust which in turn go to make road material and artificial building blocks. Very few will provide building stone, and when they do, it is often so badly 'shaken' (fissured and cracked in all directions by blasting) as to be almost worthless. Just a few quarries will allow you to select your own stone when they are not working certain benches, but on the whole you, and indeed the small contractor, must look elsewhere for supplies.

Landscape-gardening firms, garden suppliers and building contractors may be able to supply you with stone, particularly paving or cladding, or they may be able to help you to find a supplier. Right at the start insist on natural stone, and do not be put off with artificial substitutes – which always look precisely that, despite the claims of their manufacturers.

Another very good source of help is the monumental mason, particularly where special pieces of stone are required, or cutting and polishing needs to be done.

Of course, if you know where to look, you can become your own supplier. In rural areas stone has long been the traditional building material and heaps of unwanted stone cleared from fields and gardens litter the countryside. In many areas – and particularly limestone regions – small disused quarries exist with tons of good building stone scattering their floors. Establish who the owner is and ask if you can purchase some – many a farmer will be only too pleased to have the heap taken away.

City and urban dwellers need not be at a disadvantage here, either. Many old and often beautiful stone buildings are regularly demolished to make way for modern concrete-and-steel substitutes. The stone from this is a tremendous find, producing first-class 'patterned-random' walls, all the easier to build since the stone will be at least partially dressed. Keep your eyes open for such demolitions or phone local demolition contractors who, for a small fee, will often deliver a load for you. All too frequently such stone is simply dumped and covered over, but even then the effort required to locate it and sort and clean it can be well worthwhile. A haven for smaller quantities of such stone is often the council tip.

For the stoneworker planning a major project, a search for derelict buildings such as old barns and cottages can provide an abundant source of stone that will match other buildings in a particular locality. This may often be purchased at a very reasonable price from the owner. For people with old stone cottages, keep any spare stone that remains after alterations are carried out. This will be a perfect match for any later building.

Rubble and fill

Any pile of stone contains a certain amount of material that cannot be used as walling, either because it is too small or because it lacks a suitable face. This random rubble, however, is still useful and important as an infill material, either between the faces of a free-standing wall or as a base material in foundations for floors or terraces. It also provides a source of small irregularly shaped stones for *chinking* (*See* Chapter 3) or for fitting into awkward gaps that would otherwise display a large area of mortar. Thus, all the stone has a use eventually and rarely needs to be dumped.

Sorting and storing

This mainly concerns building stone that may have arrived in a mixed lorry-load or have been the fruits of your own demolition work. If you have the space, it is worth spending some time sorting the stone into a few separate piles before starting to build with it. The individual pieces can be cleaned up later as they are selected to go into the wall. With any wall there are always ends, corners, openings and so on that require a right-angled finish. Special stones termed *quoins*, with two faces at right angles to each other, are required to obtain a clean finish (Fig 8). Without experience such stones are difficult to cut but often occur either naturally or in dressed stone from old buildings.

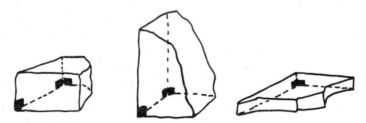

Fig 8 Some useful quoin stones – the right-angled corners are shaded

All quoins should be placed in a separate pile, and the temptation to use them in the bulk of the wall suppressed. This should be your primary concern: any stone with a right angle, whether tall and thin or short and fat, should be put into this heap. Make a second pile of very large stones, either in large block form or of paving shape; these will be important as *tie-stones* (*See* Chapter 3). The bulk of the building stone should form a third pile, with no attempt to grade for size, thus preventing areas of variation in the finished job. Finally, heap together all the small rubble and infill that can be easily shovelled into cavities as the building progresses.

When the stone is not immediately required, it should nevertheless be sorted, and stored out of the way. Thin paving stones and flagstones should be stacked on edge to prevent them being broken into tiny pieces. Someone I know stores his stone in the form of a dry wall, fulfilling a double purpose, since it also disguises an ugly bank at the bottom of his garden. He adds to and takes from this wall as and when he needs the stone somewhere else. With some thought you may find other methods of functional storage, perhaps around a compost heap or rubbish area.

Mixes

The names used to describe a mixture of cement, water, and a fine base material such as sand, dust, or powdered industrial waste vary widely. To simplify matters I have termed these, together with further mixtures that involve additions such as chippings or gravel, *mixes*. Similarly, the terms used to describe their consistency such as slack, loose, or stiff are very local and variable. I propose to avoid all these and substitute a numbered grading system from 0 to 5. Thus 0 is a completely dry mix – it contains no water at all, 5 is a very wet mix that flows off a trowel by itself.

Mixes are basically of two types: concretes, where coarse aggregates are added to the basic mix to give greater strength, and mortars, which do not include coarse aggregates. They each serve different functions.

Concretes

The addition of aggregates to a mix, providing an even distribution of particles of various sizes strongly bonded together, greatly increases strength. In stonework they are used only for the foundations of walls and paved areas and occasionally for backfilling and infilling (*See* Chapter 3). The type of aggregate used is important, the best concretes being produced from mixed sand and gravel, often termed *all-in*, where the particles are in all sizes from the microscopic to pebbles up to 2cm ($\frac{3}{4}$in) in diameter. Poor substitutes, which are simply a mixture of fine sand and 2–3cm ($\frac{3}{4}$–1$\frac{1}{8}$in) chippings, are offered as 'all-in' but produce an inferior concrete.

Basic concrete mixes and quantities are given in Table 2 of the Appendix and are generally used very wet (consistency 3–5), which enables them to be poured, and easily levelled out and smoothed off. Their slow setting further increases the hardness of the finish.

Mortars

Cement mortar may be described as the basic bonding material of both the stoneworker and the bricklayer but is used quite differently by each. The good stoneworker appreciates that well-bonded and tied stonework without mortar produces a far more attractive and stable wall than poor stonework and all the mortar in the world. All cement mixes decay after a time, and if you telescoped down the decaying time of stone to a matter of a few years, then the lifetime of the mix would be measured in seconds! Stone far outlives the mortars, all of which start to decay after about forty years.

The mortar does, however, act as a bonder, enabling walls to be less massive than when built dry. It also seals the joints between the stones, preventing invasion by plants and animals, gives a cleaner surface finish (which is important for internal work), allows a greater variety and size of stone to be used, and helps to shed water.

The mixes used have far less water than those for brickwork or concreting, usually being in the region of 1–2 for walling, but around the 2–4 mark for paving where thin paving is used. Generally, they are also mixed with a higher ratio of sand to cement than a bricklayer would use, particularly in garden work. Large proportions of cement/sand produce very hard mortars and these can lead to future problems, as over a long period of time slight earth movements produce strains in the walls. If there is joint flexibility, as provided by high ratio sand-to-cement mixes, cracking is far less likely to occur than with low ratio mixes where movement of a fraction of an inch can cause fissuring throughout the construction. Such flexibility also enables walls to cope better with weather problems (such as frost) in external work and rapid changes of temperature (such as around a fireplace) in internal work, and further emphasises the basic rule of ensuring that the stonework is correctly bonded from the start.

Various mortar mixes are given in the Appendix (Table 2), but these can be no more than a guide and, like using the trowel, the would-be stoneworker must put in a good deal of practice before gaining sufficient experience to consistently get things just right. The cardinal rule for the walling mix is not to make it too wet. Most books describe in detail the bricklayer's mortar, and this is too wet for the stoneworker. Nothing looks worse than runs and dribbles over a finished facework.

Dry mixes, type 0, are used for *grouting*; that is, for filling the joints between random paving. Their use is described in Chapter 4.

Hints on making good mixes

Regardless of whether you are mixing by hand or with a machine, a few simple points are important to achieve a good mix. Firstly, all materials must be distributed evenly throughout the mix – by hand, this is best done dry. Mixes made with materials (particularly sand) at all wet at the start often end up with the cement in little balls and are virtually useless! The sand should either be in a slurry (when using a mixer) or dry, so if you are mixing by hand keep the sand covered or bagged. It is easier to dampen the mix than to dry it out so, when adding the water at the start, be cautious: you can easily add more later. With many of the additives described in the next section, less water is required, and remember that continuously working the mix tends to make it seem wetter. Don't leave a mix turning in the machine after it has reached the consistency required. When starting off, you will tend to work slowly, so don't make a mountain of mix to last all day because it will simply 'go off' (harden) long before you've used it. Increase the size of your mixes as your skill and speed improve.

Additives

Nowadays many products are available to both improve and provide further properties in concretes and mortars for specific tasks. Many may seem expensive but are often worth the investment in the long run. No attempt will be made to describe their formulae or how they work, only to indicate what is available and what they are intended for. Many of these products are under trade names and I have a personal preference for the products of one firm for one task, and another for a different one. The products themselves and my personal recommendations will be found in Table 3 in the Appendix. Here I shall merely describe the different types of products available.

Plasticisers

For the DIY stoneworker the most important single additive is the plasticiser, and having once used it in the mortar he will be reluctant to work without it. Plasticisers make lime unnecessary, reduce the amount of water needed, but make a more malleable and workable mix that bonds well, does not flow, cleans easily, and hardens quickly. This speeds the pace of work, keeps the stone stain-free, and enables joints to be raked out, cut back, or pointed as work progresses. They also permit a greater height of walling to be built without waiting for the mixes to set below, and help to control the size of the joints. In stonework rather more plasticiser is required than is generally recommended, a fact that makes the extra expense significant. If a recommended substance is not available, ordinary washing-up liquid (which is packaged in its own handy dispenser) is a workable alternative. It must be said, though, that the long-term effects of this substitute are unknown.

Waterproofers

Mortars, even when well hardened, are porous to water, and particularly those with a high sand-to-cement ratio. Waterproofers are available that reduce the capillary movement of water between particles and also act as plasticisers. For work requiring a waterproof finish, such as ponds or the exterior facework on houses continually subjected to water invasion, a waterproofer is essential.

Hardeners

Certain additives are available that accelerate the rate of hardening of the mix. These are necessary where frost is imminent, so that work can be finished and hardened in the daytime before temperatures drop at night, or where time for hardening is otherwise limited, such as with well used floors that might have to be hardened overnight.

Colorants

Occasionally, it is desirable to change the colour of the mortar to blend in with other work, or by design as a contrast to the stone. I am not particularly fond of such contrasts but a range of colorants is produced, though most tend to fade with time.

Bonders

For certain types of work, bonders are essential and should always be used for cladding work on walls and for tiling on floors. These bonders increase the adhesion of the mortar to the stone and the cladding surface, acting like a glue. This is necessary, as the cladding work itself has no inherent support, unlike a normal wall in which the stones support each other.

Lime

Lime is the original additive of the stoneworker's mortar, although it has now been superseded by the more convenient plasticisers. I do not recommend its use by the DIY stoneworker.

3 Walling

In this chapter the basic walling techniques are described in detail and any person attempting to work in stone should try to make them second nature. They may seem complicated and awkward at the start but, like learning to drive a car, once you have mastered them they will become automatic and allow you scope to concentrate on other aspects of building when you graduate to more complex constructions later.

Walls are basically of two types: either *retaining*, where they are built to keep back a bank or change a level and thus have only one face exposed, or *free-standing*, where both faces are exposed. Generally, retaining walls are the easier for the beginner to handle but the basic principles are the same for each. Where differences occur these will be pointed out, otherwise the directions below for free-standing mortared walls apply to both.

Foundations and Footings

It may be true of a great many things that to start off properly is best, but with stonework it is absolutely essential. If you make mistakes at the start, these will be impossible to correct later without major demolition, so think out the whole project before you make a start and then stick to the plan.

Laying out the wall

In this account we shall be considering straight runs of walling – complex shapes and curves will be dealt with in Part II. The average free-standing wall along a boundary would probably be about 1m (3ft 3in) high and about 40–50cm (17–20in) thick in order to accommodate the stone for both faces and give stability. (A retaining wall would be built with its face about 30cm (12in) from the bank and then backfilled.)

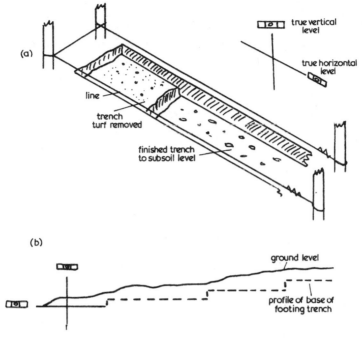

true vertical level

true horizontal level

(a)

line

trench turf removed

finished trench to subsoil level

(b)

ground level

profile of base of footing trench

Fig 9 Digging out for footings (a) a footing trench (level ground) (b) a stepped trench (sloping ground)

Having worked out where the wall is to run, firmly hammer posts into the ground at the ends of both faces of the wall and tie the lines taut between them at approximately 3cm (1⅛in) above ground level (Fig 9a). Clear the ground between the lines, keeping a look-out for any hazards such as drains, pipes, or tree stumps. If these cannot be moved or bridged, then the wall may have to be re-sited. Next remove the turves and topsoil to a depth of 10–15cm (4–6in), so that a shallow straight-sided trench is made between the lines. The base of this trench should be level. If the ground slopes naturally along the length of the projected wall, the trench should be dug out in a series of long level steps (Fig 9b).

Foundations

Generally, too much emphasis is placed on deep concrete foundations; whether these are necessary or not will become apparent when laying out the wall as above. If the base of the trench is compacted clay and stone, or even bedrock, concrete foundations are not required, and you can proceed directly with the footing course; if it is light soil or sand, the trench should be dug out a further 20cm (8in) and then filled with concrete to that depth. This base must be levelled off and allowed to set before proceeding further. Concrete foundations of such thickness are capable of supporting very large walls and, to increase their effectiveness, are made wider than the wall they support.

Footings

The first course of stonework is termed the *footings* and is always laid below ground level. This prevents the wall from being undermined by water and, should ground levels need to be altered at a later stage, foundations are not exposed. Even though this course may not be seen, it is nevertheless very important to build it correctly, for it determines the pattern of the work throughout the wall.

A layer of mortar about 5cm (2in) thick is spread along the base of the trench, the line aligned or 'trued up' along this and approximately 5–10cm (2–4in) above it. The stones are then set firmly into this mortar with their outside faces just touching (not pushed against) the lines; the outside face of each stone must be vertical at all times. Very large stones, generally about 30cm (12in) high, are placed on the outside face at intervals of about 1m (3ft 3in) with the smaller stones set between them; very large stones are also placed on the opposite face of the wall, but alternating with the ones on the other side (Fig 10a). These large stones, which I will refer to as *tie-stones* or *uprights*, have a multiple function. Firstly, because of their bulk they extend deep into the wall, and thus 'tie' or lock the two separate faces together; secondly, they act as bulwarks to build between with smaller stone, and, thirdly, they produce an even-structured pattern to a random wall that can be accentuated to a full patterned-random style if desired (Fig 15a and b).

The joints between the footing course should then be well-filled with mortar, and the spaces between the faces infilled with rubble and mortar. All is now ready for the walling proper.

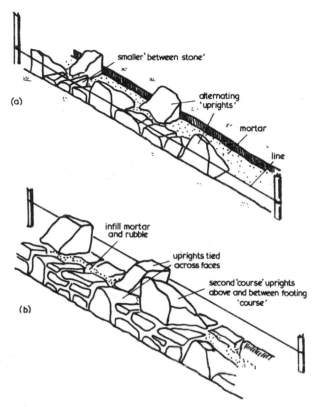

Fig 10 Arrangement of stone in (a) footings (b) subsequent random building

Building

Build to big stones

This is one of the main rules for building with random stone. If the tie-stones or uprights have been regularly and accurately placed in the footings, proceed with the walling. Use the smaller mixed building stones to fill in the gaps between the uprights (Fig 10b) to their approximate height. Try to avoid a perfect level, otherwise this will appear as a line or horizontal rift throughout the finished wall. Work one face only at a time and if, like myself, you are right-handed, you may find it more natural to move along each face from left to right.

Complete both faces in this fashion, then infill between them with rubble and mortar. The next stage is to place a new series

of uprights on the smaller building stone above and centred
between the footing series of uprights (Fig 10b) and then build
to these big stones as before. The wall thus grows in a series of
false courses determined by the uprights.

Keep the faces straight and upright by gradually raising the
line and keeping it taut as the wall grows, periodically checking
with the spirit level to ensure that it is perpendicular. If the
uprights are kept true you will soon be able to maintain
accuracy by eye between them simply by sighting along the
wall. With retaining walls the same basic procedure is used, but
only one face is worked and the wall is backfilled with rubble as
it grows.

Two-over-one, one-over-two construction

Just as brickwork and blockwork are bonded by placing the
brick or block in the next course over the joint between two in
the course below, so too must every attempt be made to bond
the joints in stonework. Thus, in stonework, one stone bridges

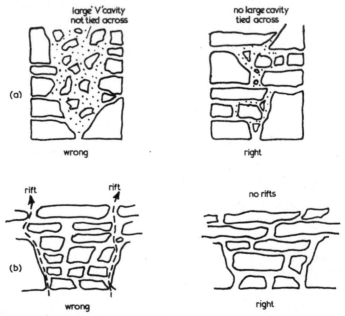

Fig 11 Ties and bonding (a) across the two faces (b) within a single face

the gap between two stones below and two stones above wherever possible (Figs 11, 32, 33). This prevents the development of long continuous mortar joints, called *vertical rifts*, running through the stone courses down the face. Such vertical rifts are the major source of weakness in stonework, and any slight settling in one part of the wall will immediately produce cracking along such rifts.

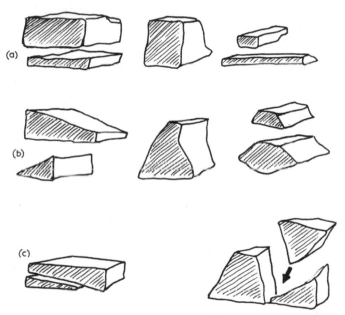

Fig 12 Basic stone shapes (faces shaded) (a) 'flat' stone (b) triangular stone (c) use of triangular stone as flat stone or triangle

Flats, triangles, and wedges

With fairly regular stone, it is simple to follow the two-over-one, one-over-two system. We, however, are concerned with random stonework where the problems are much greater. Disregarding spherical stones for the moment, your pile of building stone can be seen to be made up of three basic face shapes: flat stones, triangles, and wedges, although their sizes will vary. One type of shape may predominate; thus, if the faces are mainly squares and rectangles with fewer wedges and the odd triangle, the pile would be considered as flats (Fig 12a). If triangles predominate (including, of course, the trapezium and diamond shapes), regard the pile as being of triangles (Fig 12b) and build accordingly. Wedges can be regarded either as triangles or, when paired, as flats (Fig 12c).

With flats, maintaining the overlapped bond as described above is easy, although this should not be done in a series of perfectly level courses. With triangles and mixed stone, it is more difficult, but the same principles are involved. Lay your lower stones so that the joint between them leaves an inverted triangular space above – then simply invert a suitably sized stone into this space (Fig 12c). You will very quickly become accustomed to making the spaces accommodate the stone you have, and will thus be on your way to becoming a mason.

Laying in mortar

The technique of using the mortar is difficult to describe either in words or in a series of diagrams, so a few brief *do*'s and *don't*s must suffice. Firstly, use the trowel, not your hands – both the work and your hands will be better for it. Secondly, use plenty on the trowel and place it liberally on to the stonework so that you can work and tamp the next stone into it – another reason for keeping your mixes fairly dry and plastic. Pack the mortar well around and beneath the stone, both on the face of the wall and at the back, and press the mortar to completely fill the joints. Use the snubs of mix that fall to the ground for backing-up and infilling rather than on the face – they invariably pick up muck and stone-chips, which makes cutting out difficult.

Orientating according to shape

Owing to the infinite variability of random stone, there will often be many ways in which a piece of stone can be placed to produce different outlines on the face. Apart from purely artistic considerations, however, several other important factors have to be taken into account, which may mean that the desired face cannot be achieved. Firstly, the individual stone's top surface

Plate 5 A circular pilaster

Plate 6 A paved garden with enclosed fuel tank

Plate 7 Curves and changing levels in a steep garden

(the one at right angles to the face) must never slope downwards towards the outside of the wall but should be either level or slope inwards, where it can be built up to the level (Fig 13a and b, and *See* Chinking). Gravity will tend to pull the stone down the slope; if this slope is inwards, the wall will be pulled more tightly together; if outwards, there is nothing but the mix to prevent the stone slipping out and weakening the wall – and this will eventually and inevitably happen. Hence the initial instruction: make sure your wall would be stable without the mortar. Test your stones before fixing them in place – don't prop them in with bits of batten and board in the hope that they'll remain put when the mortar hardens!

When building up the faces, the beginner is tempted to use narrower and narrower stones, so that these rest firmly on the broader ones below. Unfortunately, this produces a V-shaped cavity between the faces and an inherent weakness along the total length of the wall (Fig 11). The infill does not particularly bind a wall; it is simply packing material that, owing to its weight, in fact exerts an outward thrust on the two wall faces. It will eventually push those faces apart if the above type of construction is used. It is important to prevent this V-cavity by using stone in a three-dimensional way, always thinking in terms of binding across the width of the wall as well as on each face. Apart from the upright ties through the construction, this can be done using long narrow stones, so that they show only a small face and their main bulk penetrates across the cavity to the other side at regular intervals (Fig 11a). If all the stone is rather small, metal ties can be used to bind the two faces together, although purists would definitely disagree with such a solution.

Similarly, it is sound stonework practice to use long flat stones in each face in order to run in a bridge across an area of small stone (Fig 11b), thus preventing vertical rifts. Such bridges are indispensable where a gap needs to be spanned or feature inserted and, if you have sorted your stone as described in Chapter 2, such bridges and ties should be readily available from the pile with the big stones.

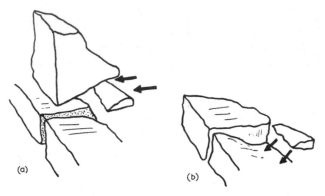

Fig 13 Chinking with stone slips to produce (a) a vertical face (b) a horizontal surface

Chinking

This is a term taken from dry-stone walling where it is used as a device for levelling up and supporting sloping stones by means of inserting small stone slips and wedges between them (Fig 13a). Where such slopes are slight, the mortar itself performs this function, but with greater slopes a stronger, more lasting result is achieved if the gaps are both chinked and mortared. If the rules above have been followed, chinking should be required only on the inside of the wall and become part of the process of infilling as the wall grows.

Stone size: wall size

A stone wall is intended to be made up of stone fitted and locked together; it is not a single row of stones with mortar between them. Thus, it is important to consider the size of the stone you use in relation to the overall height of your wall. A low garden wall, no more than 40cm (16in) high, will look ridiculous and be difficult to top off (described later) if built out of chunks of stone with faces all in excess of 25cm (10in). Similarly, tiny stone looks out of place in massive constructions. Always try to get several courses in any wall: use small and narrow stone in low walls, larger stone in higher ones.

Towards the finish

With a wall of any height you must start to think about the

finish, and prepare for it before you get there. You must ensure that the last course of uprights finishes at, or below, that height. To do this, it is easiest to mortar-in the two uprights nearest the ends of the wall to the exact finished level required, then run the line centred between them. The tightened string now represents the final level of the top of the wall and can be checked with the spirit level and, if true, topping off can proceed in an orderly manner along the wall.

Topping off

Working to a big stone as before, build up to the line, keeping the final stone level along it. The uprights should now all be set to reach the line wherever possible. Thus, if smallish, they should be raised by building up with a smaller flattish stone beneath rather than placing a thin stone as the last stone over the upright. Small thin stones are very easily knocked loose from the top of walls (unless a coping is added), and every effort should be made to avoid a line of thin stones at the topping-off stage. For topping off, the mortar should probably be slightly richer and wetter than the basic building mix (*See* Appendix Table 2).

When both faces are completed, infilling is determined by the type of finish required. If the wall is to be surmounted by a coping, infilling continues with rubble and mortar as before, the last 8–10cm (3–4in) being finished off level with either mortar or concrete. If the top of the wall is going to be left open and planted, the inside of each face should be well backed with mortar in order to leave a trough of some 20–25cm (8–10in) deep that can then be filled with soil or compost.

Ending the wall (*See* Chapter 6)

Slopes

Regardless of the slope of the ground, stonework and the individual stones should be kept level wherever the stone has a pronounced horizontal edge. If the footings have been correctly stepped as shown in Fig 9b, maintaining the level is simple, and the temptation to lay stone, particularly flattened rectangular

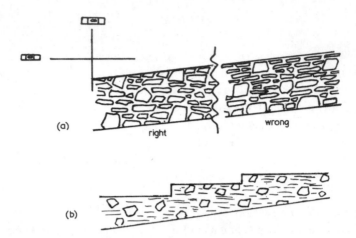

Fig 14 Finishing on a slope (a) correct and incorrect orientation for a sloping wall (b) stepped top to a sloping wall

stone, parallel with the slope should be resisted. Figure 14a indicates how stone of different shapes should be aligned, and this does not really require a spirit level and plumb bob. The balance mechanism of our bodies tends to keep us automatically upright, regardless of slope; our two eyes provide us with the horizontal line to this vertical axis. We can all easily tell if a pillar leans or a picture is crooked. So, if you stand back and look at the work regularly as building progresses, similar faults will be obvious. By concentrating on it from the start, the selection and correct placement of stone will become automatic.

If a wall is to be finished to a slope, say to maintain a fixed height in relation to a falling pavement (Fig 14), the topping-off stones may be sloped, but it is generally better to use wedge shapes. A long steep slope, however, may be accommodated by finishing the wall in a series of horizontal steps (Fig 14b).

Patterns and contrasts

If desired, the walling may be constructed to produce a patterned effect within the random concept. A contrast between the uprights and smaller stone can be accentuated by selecting long, flattened, horizontal stones for building between the ties (Fig 15b). The degree to which such patterning is

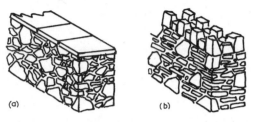

Fig 15 Building styles (a) full random stonework (b) markedly 'patterned' random stonework. Note also the different copings

stressed is simply a matter of careful placement and matching of the uprights and contrasting of the 'between stone'. Where flat stone is less available, such patterning will be less marked. Personal designs, symbols, and motifs can simply be built into the wall by using a contrasting material, such as slate with limestone, to accentuate them (Plate 3).

Retaining walls

Retaining walls are approached in the same way as free-standing walls unless they are built more than about 1m high, when other considerations may be involved. A tall retaining wall is subjected to great pressures from both the soil or rubble it holds back, and from the water that may build up behind it in wet weather. Greater strength can be given by building the wall to a *batter*, meaning that instead of the face being perfectly vertical, it is sloped slightly backwards into the bank (Fig 16).

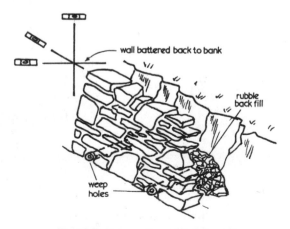

wall battered back to bank

rubble
back fill

weep
holes

Fig 16 Features of a retaining wall

This is achieved by setting each stone slightly back from the stone beneath, while keeping its individual face vertical; *not* by sloping the individual stones themselves, which would eventually produce a bulge in the base of the wall. To prevent water building up behind the wall, 'weep holes' are left. This is most conveniently done by building in piping at an angle through the base of the wall and backfilling with rubble to allow the water to percolate freely downwards and then run out through the piping (Fig 16).

Cutting building stone (*See* Chapter 5)

Finishes

The wall may be regarded as complete at the end of the topping-off stage. It can, however, be further embellished by the addition of a coping.

Copings

Copings are of many different styles and perform different functions, but may be broadly divided into two main groups: flat coping and raised coping. Both types are set in wetter and richer mortar than is used for walling. Bonders can be incorporated into the mix for extra adhesion.

Fig 17 Laying a flat cement mortar coping

Flat coping

Apart from giving a neat uniform finish to walls, flat copings further tie the two faces together, prevent dislodgement of the topping-off stones, assist in waterproofing the wall, and can convert low walls into convenient seats. One simple way of producing such a coping is from a proofed mortar mix trowelled smooth and levelled between a timber frame to slightly overlap the faces (Fig 17). Other copings can be made out of concrete slabs cut to overlap, or, alternatively, the wall may be built to the right thickness to accommodate standard-sized slabs, such as 45cm (18in) or 60cm (24in). Perhaps the best (but most expensive) coping is of cut and polished slate or stone, but normally this would be considered only for special features such as barbecue and seating areas.

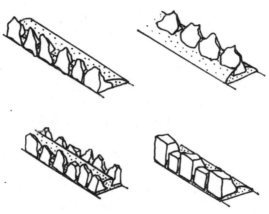

Fig 18 Some raised coping styles

Raised copings

Raised copings are produced out of random stone and provide an opportunity for using up the awkward pointed pieces that defeated you in the actual walling work. They further raise the wall height to anything from 22cm (9in) to 30cm (12in) with little additional effort. Raised copings are generally laid along the centre of the wall or along one face only – the outer face – and the mortar sloped down to the other face to shed water (Fig 18). The different styles used, and their names, are legion, ranging from the informal 'ragged copings' (Fig 18, top row, and bottom row left) to the alternate up-and-down formality of the 'cock-and-hen' (Fig 18 bottom row right). Style is a matter of choice, but whichever one is adopted remember that the stones will vary in size, so randomise the copings, thus preventing all tall stones at one end and short at the other with a resulting slope between them.

Pointing

Although pointing has been left to this section, attention to the joints should really continue right through the building phase, with only certain types of pointing being left until the wall is completed. Like copings, joint finishes can be separated into two categories: 'cut back' or 'raised'. Some general considerations, however, are pertinent to both and will be discussed first. Pointing and jointwork should enhance the stonework, not obscure it, and personally I consider this to be its most important function. Books on brickwork pay great attention to the shaping of the pointing as a water-shedding device. Water penetration through mortar porosity, however, is generally unimportant in stonework owing to waterproofing additives and the thickness of the construction, whereas in 22cm (9in) brickwork damp penetration may be very important.

Cut-back pointing

The beauty of stonework, particularly random work, is in the stone and the way in which it is laid; the jointwork should endeavour to enhance this, not mask it. The way to make pointing highlight your stonework is either to rake out or cut back the mortar joints before the mortar has fully set, thus creating shadows that emphasise the stone (Fig 19). It has to be done as work progresses and the surplus snubs, smudges, and the top centimetre of mix can either be scraped away to leave a hollow effect (Fig 19b) or cut with the pointing tool to leave a central pointed ridge through the joint exactly following the outline of the stones (Fig 19c). A wall without attention to the joints is a mark of either laziness or inexperience, and in both cases more often than not accompanies poor building work in general. In some cases, workmen brush out the joints while they are still damp to produce a smooth finish. This reduces

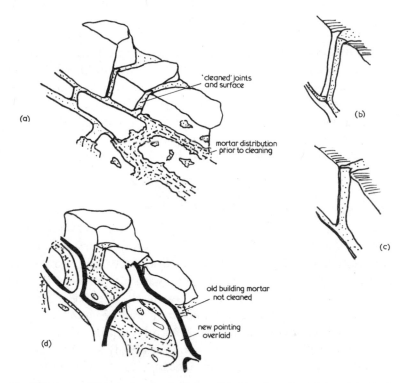

Labels in figure:
(a)
'cleaned' joints and surface
mortar distribution prior to cleaning
(b)
(c)
(d)
old building mortar not cleaned
new pointing overlaid

Fig 19 Pointing (a) cleaning up the joints (b) ridged cut-back joints (c) raked-out joints (d) snail-creep raised pointing

shadows and disguises the stone; its sole merit is speed. No DIY person should need to sacrifice craftmanship for speed.

Raised pointing

Raised pointings are laid on to stonework after the walling has been completed, and generally overlay smoothed-out joints. Various styles are adopted, from those fairly faithfully following the original joints to the wiggly lines called *snail-creep* that wander over the face in a manner bearing no relation to the actual stonework (Fig 19d). Their only excuse can be to disguise poor workmanship beneath.

Dealing with round stones

I do not recommend the DIY enthusiast to use round stones unless he has to. They tend to produce weaker walls because of the difficulty of tying in within the faces, and it is impossible to produce angles and corners with them. In addition, hybrid walls incorporating both round and angular stone tend to look a mess. Where they are used, however, they are always set in the gap between two stones below, on a good bed of mortar. Because the greatest width of the stone is at its centre, the mortar joints are wide and must be cut well back.

Dry Walling

Although I have restricted myself to discussing mortared stone walls, another type of construction technique, dry walling, is commonly associated with stonework. Here the stones are fitted together, and the walls built, without the assistance of cement or lime mortars. This is obviously the oldest form of walling, having been employed long before mortars were discovered. Dry work, however, generally requires greater skill than mortared work. Dry walls are not simply a heap of stones haphazardly dumped together, nor are true dry walls the type of small retaining wall associated with a change of level in sloping gardens. Real dry walling can be seen in upland areas of Britain such as the Lake and Peak Districts, where free-standing walls of significant proportions have been constructed without using any form of packing material. As the average reader is unlikely to be interested in building walls like these I shall restrict my discussion of dry walling to garden stone walls built without the use of mortar.

Limitations of dry walling

Dry walling can only be used in certain areas and for certain jobs, so is less flexible than mortared stonework. It cannot be used in constructional building, for complex work, nor inside the home, and so it is restricted to rather simple projects in the garden. For most people dry stonework requires good regularly shaped stones, generally of a paving shape laid flat. Without good stone and considerable skill, large free-standing walls cannot be built, and dry work is mainly confined to fairly small retaining walls.

Dry walling is relatively impermanent, the stones being dislodged easily or moved by mechanical damage or weather action; they thus require regular maintenance. The open joints are a haven for all types of animal life, particularly slugs, snails, and the pupae of many insects. Thus, garden dry walls encourage pests, whereas mortared walls offer very little scope for invasion.

Advantages of dry walling

Dry walling is both quick and cheap to build compared with mortared walls, because it requires neither the materials and additives nor the time in which to prepare the mortar. For the same reasons it is less messy and takes up less garden space. There are no drainage problems associated with dry retaining walls, as water works its way naturally through the open joints.

Dry walls in the garden can be made most attractive by arranging plants in the wall face between the joints. This planting can be altered or undertaken over a period of time, unlike mortared walls where fixed planting pockets must be left in the face.

Building hints

Only build a dry wall where it is sensible – most commonly for garden and boundary retaining walls. Do not build on concrete foundations but set the footing stones below ground level. Always build to a batter; that is, slope the face back by setting the stones a little farther in each time. Strictly obey the rules for walling such as overlapping the joints, building to a big stone, and tying-in. Use clean, dry, fine earth between the stones, dumping each trowel-full above the lower joint and spreading it outwards over the stone. Wherever possible plant the wall as you build, spreading the plant roots out; this will benefit both the wall and the plants. It takes time for a wall to 'settle', so do delay the topping-off as long as possible. Top off with larger thicker stone: it will be harder to dislodge than small thin pieces.

More detailed accounts of dry-wall construction can be found in some gardening books.

4 Paving and Cladding

Paving and cladding are included in a single chapter because of the similarities in the basic materials used for them and the relationships between them. All quantities for various types of paving and cladding materials are provided in an area/weight relationship table in the Appendix (Table 1). Some suppliers nowadays do sell the more expensive materials, such as decorative slates for cladding, by the square metre or yard. In this way, ordering is simplified even if you do have to pay extra.

Paving

Compared with cladding, random-stone paving calls for an entirely different approach to walling, since it deals with extensive areas in the horizontal instead of the vertical plane and, of course, uses entirely differently shaped materials. Genuine stone paving is now very difficult to obtain, and often expensive – though I consider it worth the extra cost and effort. I have, therefore, included information on dealing with broken concrete paving slabs, such as may be obtained cheaply from local council highway departments. When subjected to weathering, such slabs lose some of their harshness. Coloured, regular concrete slabs, however, have no place in a book on random stonework and are thus not included.

Like walling, paving may be permanently laid in a mortar mix or put down 'dry' in earth or sand. A description of how to construct dry paving will be found later. Constructional and design techniques also vary, depending on whether external terraces and patios, paths, internal floors, or steps are being considered. The basic techniques involved in all such paving work will be examined in the following section on terraces and patios. In addition, special notes on paths are dealt with at the end of the chapter, and on floors and steps in Chapters 8 and 9.

Terraces and patios

Since the words 'terrace' and 'patio' seem today to be interchangeable, and the constructional techniques for each identical, I shall regard both as essentially external areas covered with a hard and durable surface material – in this instance, random-stone paving.

Laying out the terrace

Unlike walls, which in small gardens tend to follow predetermined boundaries, terraces are usually sited within the garden and the owner can thus use his design talents. Design considerations cannot be examined here in detail but a few words about the materials used might prove useful. The very fact that you are dealing with randomly shaped materials allows full flexibility of the total construction shape without the need for complex cutting and the like. This provides an opportunity to get away from straight lines and, by using curves, to change the whole appearance of a narrow rectangular plot.

Having decided on the basic overall design, the next consideration should be the proposed final level of a finished terrace. Unlike an interior floor, garden terraces are open to rain, and an ill-concieved patio can become a shallow pool or mud-bath very quickly, while water lying against the walls of a house will quickly cause damp problems. All external paved areas should fall very slightly, and the slightest gradient (say, 1:1,000) will suffice to drain away the water, while retaining a level appearance. Wherever possible the direction of fall should be away from the house; otherwise the water must be collected into a gutter and channelled into a drain and soakaway that need to be planned and excavated in advance.

Where paving is to butt up against the house, the finished level must be below the damp-proof course, preferably at least 7cm (3in) below it. The damp-proof course can be identified as a black felt or bitumen strip running around the house just below outside door level.

During this initial laying-out stage, other potential problems must also be noted and taken into account regarding the proposed final levels. Near houses, drains, pipes and inspection-covers are common, and often metre-wide concrete paths rigidly girdle the dwelling. Drains must normally be left open and can be used to get rid of surplus water from the terrace. Inspection-cover levels can easily be altered and often disguised. Concrete paths, however, cause special problems. Wherever possible, these should be removed or covered; nothing looks so out of place as random-stone paving butted up to an old concrete path! If you have been fortunate enough to obtain rivings (*See* Materials page 36) and if the damp-proof course is sufficiently above the concrete path, you may safely pave over the concrete without actual excavation, and run the terrace out into the garden from this level. With thicker material – say 4–6cm (1½–2½in) paving – the concrete path must be broken up and removed, so that a new level can be created. The concrete itself, however, may come in useful as a hardcore fill beneath your new terrace.

Having coped with the above list of possible problems you can proceed with the task of actually building your terrace. The ground should first be cleared of any vegetation over an area slightly bigger than the proposed terrace, and roughly raked. This organic material should be burnt or composted and never used for fill, because it will rot with time, contract, and cause sinking in places. If the terrace is to be regular in outline, its boundaries can easily be marked out with pegs and string. Where the outline is curved, it is easiest to lay a thick trail of sand along the proposed boundary. Stand back and view it as a whole and alter the trail to produce an even flowing line. This can then be marked more permanently by driving pegs into the ground at intervals of approximately 60cm (2ft).

Preparation of the site

How you tackle the preparatory stage will depend on whether the site has to be excavated in order to lower it to an existing level, or raised to a new level. In many cases, where the ground slopes, it will be a combination of both, excavated material from high ground being used as fill in the lower levels. Where the paving butts the house, the ground must be excavated well below the damp-proof course to accommodate the hardcore and rubble fill. To work out the depth of excavation, allow approximately 10cm (4in) for coarse rubble and hardcore, 3–5cm (1–2in) for the mortar, and allow also for the thickness of the paving material used. Thus, with broken concrete paving the initial level should be some 20cm (8in) below the proposed finishing level. This is purely a guide for average soil conditions; where the ground is stony subsoil, the hardcore layer may be dispensed with and the ground levelled out at half the above depth.

Hardcore may be purchased as such, but any solid material can be substituted. If you have been walling, you will already possess rubble waste, rock chips, and old mortar snubs that can be used. Existing concrete paths can be broken up, and in new houses obliging builders always seem to donate to the aspiring gardener a vast collection of broken blocks and bricks in addition to the ubiquitous plastic sheeting, electrical wire, and empty paint tins. Whatever base-fill you use, make sure that it is packed down hard, so that any future settling is minimised. The air spaces between the coarse lumps can be filled with soil worked well in to prevent future movement.

Some people consider this base satisfactory for paving, but by experience I have found that a layer of fine material, such as gravel or 2cm and smaller ($\frac{3}{4}$inch down) chippings, greatly assists and speeds the work later. This is simply barrowed on to the site and raked over it. If battens are pegged across the site and levelled off (Fig 22), these chippings can be raked out of these levels, and problems with dips and bumps at a later stage are immediately eliminated. The chippings are also able to accommodate those rare, but annoying, thick chunks of stone that occur with stone paving and cannot easily be split off.

Laying the paving

Never attempt to lay paving in wet weather or with wet stone – the object is to keep the stone clean, and smears and smudges of cement on expensive decorative stone are extremely difficult to remove.

Paving can be bedded into either a wet-mortar mix or a dry

one (one without any water added). Although the latter
method is both quicker and easier, the result is less satisfactory,
particularly when stone of varying thickness is used. Mortar
shrinks when dampened, and this can lead to unevenness in the
terrace; it does not bond as well to the paving as wet mortar and
is thus totally unsatisfactory for thin riven stone. The DIY
stoneworker should therefore bed the paving permanently in a
wet mix. (*See* Appendix Table 2) in most instances. The mortar
is laid in a full bed beneath the pavings and not in dabs at the
corners as recommended in some books, which produces
hollows beneath the stone and always results in cracking where
thin riven paving is used.

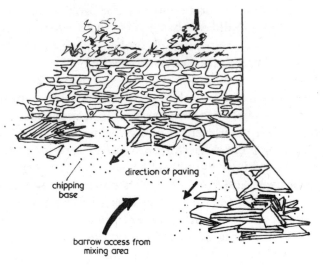

Fig 20 Direction of paving

The starting point for paving is also important. A fixed level
such as against the house, would make a good starting point.
The direction you pave depends on access to the site; in other
words, the route from mixer or mixing area to the paving. The
barrow must not be wheeled across freshly laid paving, but over
the chippings – here the ballbarrow is indispensable – and up to
the working edge, where it can be tipped on to the desired area

(Fig 20). Try and envisage it as a room in which you are painting the floor – you want to end up at the doorway, not trapped on the other side of the room!

The slabs should be of random sizes; it is often tempting to lay large pieces first and fit tiny pieces round them, then end up with whatever is left over. Avoid doing this. Also try to avoid laying long straight edges against others and then infilling the gaps; instead, lay points into the gaps so that the whole terrace locks together like a jigsaw puzzle (Fig 21a). Similarly, try to prevent long rifts occurring in the terrace as with walling, especially where the area is large and the work has to proceed in stages. Rifts will divide the finished job up into separate visual compartments (Fig 21b). If the job has to be left incomplete, clean up any surplus mortar right to the exposed edge of the paving before it hardens. Attempting to cut it away with lump hammer and chisel at a later stage will tend to loosen or even crack the slabs.

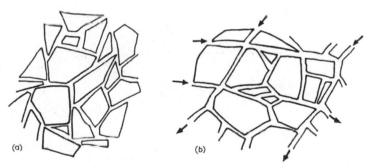

Fig 21 Laying the paving slabs (a) fully interlocked with no rifts (b) laid in discrete compartments producing long rifts

If you are also considering making steps or straight edges to paths or borders, it is worthwhile to reserve a quantity of slabs from the start with both good right angles and long, clean, straight edges for the subsequent jobs. This will avoid the complication of having to cut stone at a later stage.

Some books recommend that you lay out your paving over the whole site and fit the pieces together before you actually start to bed them in. People who recommend this method cannot have laid many terraces. The paving gets in the way of the barrow; it has to be moved aside to put down the mortar bed; pieces inevitably get broken; and if you can lay it out loose you can obviously bed it while you're doing so.

Keeping the levels

Final levels can be maintained in two ways. A small looped peg, such as a skewer, can be driven in at fixed points where paving begins and, some distance away, a batten set in mortar at the finished level. A string from the skewer pulled tight across the batten can be moved in an arc across the paving area (Fig 22). This ensures that you keep your paving at a fixed falling level just below the string. It is a very easy permanent method of keeping the work smooth and true, but the simpler method of using a long board and the spirit level (making a new mark to allow for the displacement of the bubble owing to the drainage slope) can also be used.

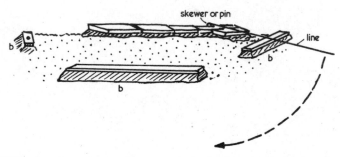

Fig 22 Keeping the paving to the required level by means of a line moved in an arc over the battens (b) set in the mortar at the finished height

Without considerable experience, difficulties will occur in judging the exact amount of mortar required beneath stone of varying thickness, so the bed will have to be reduced or built up as required. Where a paving stone is only slightly raised above its neighbours it may legitimately, be tamped down to the level of the other stones. To do this, either use the handle of the lump hammer, provided it is not wooden as it would then split and curl, or the wooden head of the pick handle. Tamping should be done with several gentle blows all over the surface of the stone and never with the metal head of the hammer or by a few mighty blows in the centre of the stone as this would simply crack it.

Grouting

Grouting the joints as you go along with the bedding mix generally results in smears at the edges of the paving, and is very time-consuming. I prefer to grout in areas of completed paving with a *dry* grouting mix (*See* Appendix Table 2) that is scattered over the stone, then brushed into the joints tightly with a soft broom. The stone must be perfectly dry but the mortar bed still not hardened, so that the grout immediately draws moisture from it, bonds with it, and sets quickly. If grouting is left until the terrace is completed and the bed set, the dry mix hardens slowly, bonds badly, and often gets blown or scratched away, leaving grooves between the stones and an uneven surface. Surplus grout can be scattered over the chippings at the end of each day – it is not advisable to store it unless you can keep it really dry and airtight.

Finishes

Like walls, paving can be enhanced by attention to detail and to the finish. Often, large areas of paving can look drab and should be broken up. This can be done by leaving out slabs in order to provide small planting pockets for low-growing plants that add life and colour. Spaces for plants at paving level, or raised by means of a low wall, can further reduce the monotony. Otherwise, areas of paving can be laid in materials that contrast with the main paving stone, for instance, circles of coloured slate with limestone surrounds.

Where a terrace is raised, the paving should lip a few centimetres over the retaining wall, and the mortar be cleaned off beneath as for walling. This casts a shadow and increases the depth of the work. With such lipping, the outer edges of the paving should touch to prevent a 'gappy' appearance.

Obstructions

Obstructions fall into two categories: man-made and natural. The commonest in the first group is the inspection cover. Nature's own methods of disguise include making something so much larger than normal that the mind considers it impossible to be what it actually is, or to blend it so skilfully with its surroundings that the senses do not register it at all. We can use the same disguises for our obstructions and eye-sores.

Unfortunately, inspection covers serve an important function and must remain accessible, so cannot be paved over in the normal manner. The most satisfactory method of treatment is to lower them well below the finished paving level (this is done by simply knocking off one course of bricks and refitting the cover and frame) and pave right up to them. A single slab of paving stone may then be cut to size (*See* Chapter 5) and bedded in pure sand to level with the surrounding paving. To mark the position, a large planted pot or even some item of garden furniture may be placed on the slab. Simply setting a pot on the inspection cover itself only draws attention to the cover.

The most common natural hazards are trees and outcrops of bedrock. In each case, you should draw attention to them, so that the observer believes that they are an integral focal point of the design. With trees, leave a clear-cut circle of soil at least 60cm (2ft) around the trunk and plant with massed flowering plants, or build in a seat round the tree. With rock outcrops, break away part of the sloping shoulders, and then pave to leave planting areas, but combine evergreens which give height and spread and soften the sudden change in level – and flowering Alpines that look natural with a rocky background and add interest and colour.

Cutting and splitting paving (*See* Chapter 5)

Special considerations

Terraces quickly become functional as well as decorative areas, and this should be borne in mind from the start. A good terrace dries out fast after rain and is readily swept and cleaned, and is thus able to fill the roles of a children's playground, an afternoon tea, sunbathing, or barbecue area. The widespread variety of uses to which it can be put is a measure of the care and skill with which it was planned and then built. So please do not permanently cement the rotary clothes-line in the centre of it; site it to one side and make it removable. If the terrace is raised and surrounded by a wall (*See* Plate 11), make sure that water can easily drain through that wall, otherwise you will have a paddling pool rather than a terrace. If you are going to have steps leading to a raised terrace, don't automatically centre them – another place might be more functional and effective.

Paths

Laying a path with random stone is basically the same as building a patio, but there are one or two features that are more important, and influence the final quality of the work. In considering design, remember that a path running in a straight line from gate to door immediately divides the garden into two separate narrow strips. Let your paths curve and wander around features in the manner of a stream, but do not exaggerate the curves to such an extent that everyone takes short cuts over your carefully tended borders or lawn!

When building paths, ensure that the foundations are good and make all slopes even and gentle. Where steep gradients have to be overcome, they can be lessened by looping a path across the gradient and also by using steps. Steeply sloping garden paths are dangerous in wet weather for young and old alike. The paths should also be of a good width, rarely narrower than 50cm (21in), so that they can accommodate pram and pushchair as well as the garden barrow and lawn mower.

The width is also important to allow linked building. With narrow paths, single slabs may stretch across the total width, leaving a series of straight lines across the path. Avoid this and keep the edges strong by laying good-sized slabs along the outside of the path and tapering inwards; then inlay with small stone down the spine of the path (Fig 23a). However, if a path is bounded on both sides by a wall – that is, if it is sunken in relation to its boundaries – the opposite rule applies, since the walls confine the path. In this case, the larger slabs are laid

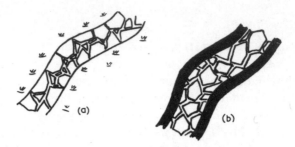

Fig 23 Paving paths (a) with a grass boundary – largest slabs to the outside (b) with a raised wall boundary – largest slabs to the centre

down the spine of the path, where there is the most wear, and the small stones infilled to butt up against the retaining walls (Fig 23b). It often happens that a path is bounded by a wall on one side only. In this case, common sense will determine how the two principles may be combined in practice.

Finally, in all cases, keep the centre of the path very slightly higher than the edges, so that water is easily shed.

Steps and floors (See Chapter 4)

Dry paving

Random paving may be laid in the garden entirely without mortar. A more informal effect is obtained by setting the slabs in soil to allow for plant growth between the stones.

The principles of fitting, levelling, and laying out the area are much the same as for mortared terraces. After the proposed terrace area has been dug out, it should be raked level, and a heap of light, dry, sieved soil stacked on one side. The base of the terrace must then be consolidated, packing it down hard to prevent subsidence later. Paving is done with a slightly thicker stone than that used in a mortared terrace. Lay the stones in an equal mix of sand and soil, and grout between the slabs with a similar sand-soil mix.

Unevenness will always occur in dry paved areas as a result of underground root and soil movement, and cannot be prevented. A degree of unevenness does not necessarily look out of place in a dry terrace, however, especially when the area has become well established with plants.

Cladding

There is some doubt as to whether or not stone cladding can really be regarded as true stonework since it is more akin to tiling with randomly shaped stone tiles than anything else. Its main function is to cover an ugly finish beneath, and perhaps persuade the uncritical eye that it is really built out of stone. Carried out properly, it can also provide a very effective method of waterproofing external surfaces. Since I do not consider cladding to be stonework in the true sense, I shall not consider it in very great detail.

Preparation of the surface

Clad stones, like tiles, are not self-supporting, therefore they must adhere firmly and permanently to the supporting structure. If the latter is cracked, they will simply pull loose render away, so some degree of surface preparation is essential.

Hack off old render unless it is very sound; patch in loose brickwork; and ensure that the surface is dust- and grease-free – use a stabilising compound if necessary where old joints are of crumbly lime mortar. If the surface is very smooth, for example, in the case of glazed bricks, it may be necessary to rough this up first to provide a good key for the adhesive.

Fixing the stone

The stone can be fixed either by the addition of a bonding agent such as 'Unibond' or 'Febond' to an ordinary mortar mix (*See* Appendix, Table 3), or by a special ready-prepared adhesive. For the DIY person, the latter method is probably the safest, even if rather more expensive, and bonders such as 'Febtile' waterproof mortar are specifically developed for exterior stone claddings. These are almost foolproof, completely waterproof, and carry full directions for use.

Unlike artificial tiles, stone varies slightly in thickness, and too wide a range will make cladding almost impossible. If you are going to clad, purchase ready-sorted cladding from a good supplier at 9mm–13mm ($\frac{3}{8}$–$\frac{1}{2}$in) thick. This will avoid a lot of sorting and splitting, with the attendant wastage, or the rough-

and-ready result of a make-do approach.

Work in the maximum length of run, and don't attempt to achieve great heights before the lower courses are well set. Any slumping will require repetition of the whole job. Apply the mix to the surface as directed by the makers of the bonder, and paint the back of the stone with the adhesive as well. Make sure that the joints between the individual stones are of even width, cutting the stone (*See* Chapter 5) where necessary. The width of joint called for is a matter of preference and can be regulated with slips of wood inserted between the stones, removed as the mix hardens. Many people find it easier, however, to ignore separated joints at this stage and butt the stone as tightly as possible to its neighbour. When the work is complete, a new joint of even thickness is pointed up over the cracks and disguises the slight joint variation that is inevitable with irregular stone.

Keep the surface of the stone clean and free of adhesive as you go – unpolished stone is very difficult to clean afterwards, and badly smeared pieces should be discarded or washed thoroughly clean before the smears harden, then allowed to dry before being used again. (It is, incidentally, impossible to undertake good cladding work in the rain.)

5 Working Stone

This is a miscellaneous chapter in which numerous 'odds and ends' of techniques and problems encountered when working with natural stone are grouped together. It also includes some hints on cutting and splitting stone and when not to do so, as well as moving, lifting, and shaping awkward chunks.

Splitting and Cutting Stone

Splitting
Since both sedimentary and metamorphic rocks are formed in layers, like wood they possess a 'grain' corresponding to these layers and, like wood, can be split along the line of the grain if this is sufficiently regular and distinct.

Whenever you intend to split a block of stone, it is most important that you examine it from all angles to find the exact line of the grain and to see whether or not it runs true through the block (parallel to the face you require, Fig 24). Minor disturbances and pressures during the formation of the rock can lead to changes in the angles of the grain of the solidified rock. If you attempt to split a block where this has happened you will end up with only odd fillets of stone rather than the desired sheets. To further complicate matters, angled and straight grain sections may both occur in the same piece of stone!

Where the grain is pronounced, splitting is simple and requires the use of only the bolster, cold chisel, and lump hammer. With very large blocks the sledgehammer, together with steel wedges, may prove useful.

Starting the split is most important – do not place the bolster at one end and simply hammer away! Work the bolster along the whole length of the intended split hammering it down at approximately 15cm (6in) intervals until a straight crack

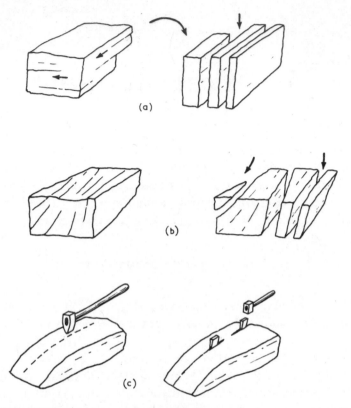

Fig 24 Splitting stone (a) regular straight-grained blocks (b) twisted grained stone (c) large stone, using a mason's hammer and wedges

appears along the length of the grain (Fig 24c). Then you can progressively widen this crack until the slab you require breaks free.

Such stone is most easily split along the natural crack or layers that appear in the grain, for these are lines of weakness. Often, however, although the grain can be identified, there appears to be no natural place to start splitting off and a slightly different technique is called for. Here the large mason's hammer, either in the single-handed or sledgehammer version, comes into its own. Strike along the grain at intervals as before, but directly and forcefully with the shaped part of the hammer head, and keep repeating the blows at the same points until a hairline crack appears along the grain. This crack may then be exploited with bolster or wedges as before. This method is the most effective way of obtaining thicker chunks of more compact stone for building rather than paving.

Cutting

Often it is necessary to cut stone, particularly paving, across the line of the grain at an angle in order to reduce its size or make it fit an awkward gap. With regard to cutting stones to fill awkward gaps when paving, my advice is: don't try it unless absolutely essential. Instead, use smaller pieces. Sometimes a piece of stone must be cut to produce a clean straight edge or right angle, and this can be done either by hand or with a stone-cutter.

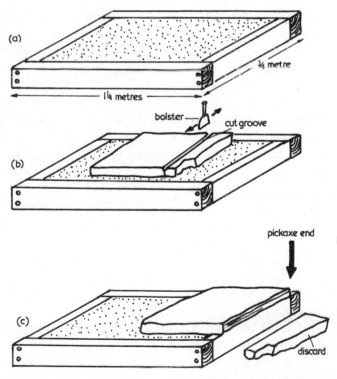

Fig 25 Hand cutting a paving slab at right angles to the grain (a) a sand box (b) cutting the groove (c) breaking the slab

Hand-cutting

The main DIY tools for hand-cutting paving stone are the bolster and lump hammer, and if a lot of cutting is needed it may be worthwhile to construct a sand box (Fig 25a), which will serve as a cushion to absorb the hammer blows. Otherwise, a smooth bed of sand and a stout straight piece of timber (or angle iron) can be used.

Mark out the line to be cut by scoring a mark with the corner of the bolster using a straight edge of timber, then bed the slab firm and level on the sand. Work up and down along the line with hammer and bolster until a definite groove is cut – the deeper the better, and at least one-fifth of the thickness of the slab. Pay particular attention to the edges of the stone, cutting a deep V-notch on each side through the whole thickness of the slab (Fig 25b). Move the slab on to the timber so that the groove lies directly above its edge, with the worked portion still firmly bedded on the sand, and the discard portion clear of the ground (Fig 25c). Strike the discard portion sharply and firmly with the base of a pick while anchoring the slab with your foot. A clean break should occur along the groove, any slight irregularities being easily nibbled away with the chisel end of the small mason's hammer. Where the discard portion is very narrow, it may not be possible to break it off cleanly with the pick base. In this instance, keep the slab firm on the timber and work along the discard strip with the lump hammer breaking off sections at a time.

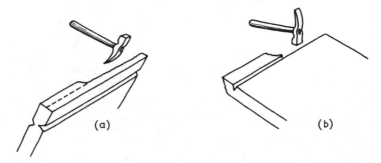

Fig 26 Cutting concrete slab or soft stone (a) the undercut (b) the finish

A different technique is used to shape and cut old concrete paving. The small mason's hammer alone is employed and fairly complex profiles may be produced with ease. Mark out the finished line as above; then strike at the under edge of the slab with the chisel end of the hammer undercutting the face (Fig 26). The face may then be knocked off cleanly with the hammer from above, and the process repeated until the mark is reached. For cutting long straight edges in concrete slabs use the same technique as described above for stone – the softer material makes this rather easier. This undercutting technique can also be used with softish limestones.

With the harder metamorphic rocks, such as slate, cutting across the grain to produce a clean edge is far more difficult since these rocks tend to shatter. Hand cutting such stone is complex and laborious if thicknesses of more than 12mm ($\frac{1}{2}$in) are used, and is not really within the scope of this DIY book. Take your slab, marked out, to a firm specialising in cutting stone and sit back while they do it for you.

Stone-cutters

Mechanical stone-cutters are a boon where a lot of cross-grain cutting is required, and eliminate the effort involved with hammer and bolster. The basic principles are precisely the same as for hand cutting, the only difference being that the marked groove is made by a revolving disc instead of by a bolster – breaking off the discard is the same as before. A couple of hints on using these cutters, however, may make their use not only easier but more effective.

Their discs revolve very rapidly in a direction away from the operator, so draw the disc along the mark towards you – never attempt to use it in the opposite direction, you might take off! Draw the disc with light pressure along the mark in one single sweep to start with, then increase the pressure and move the cutter more slowly on subsequent sweeps. It will naturally follow the first groove you have made. Never bear down hard on the machine: you *won't* cut any more stone, you *will* reduce the life of the disc!

The machine produces a great deal of stone dust and intense

heat so, after the initial mark has been made, run a hosepipe on the stone; the water will reduce the amount of dust and increase the life of the cutting discs by helping to keep them cool.

These stone-cutters cannot be used for cutting slates – they generate too much heat and split off the surface. For slate you need a special water-cooled saw, at present not generally available from hire firms. Do not risk expensive stone; take it to experts – they charge for the risks.

Working Building Stone

Pitching and dressing building stone successfully requires a combination of both art and craftmanship, and any attempt to persuade the DIY enthusiast that after reading this book he will be competent to take on these jobs would be foolhardy. This short section is simply to tempt readers into 'having a go', for only then will you discover whether or not you have the necessary feel for the work and the desire to go further and use stone in more creative and demanding ways. I trust that professional masons will forgive my cursory treatment of this most important aspect of their work and appreciate that some aspects of their trade cannot be taught through books.

The main problem confronting the stoneworker attempting to shape a stone – to produce a particular angle for instance – is the nature of the stone itself. Every stone is an 'individual' with its own particular character and must suit the work required of it. Try to work with the stone, in other words, not against it. For example, stone with folded grain and faults will not produce a good right angle for corner work unless it is sawn.

Fortunately, with random work little pitching is required – the beauty of the finish being largely in the *lack* of uniformity of the individual stones. And so this section is devoted mainly to improvement of the face of the stone and to the production of quoins, or cornerstones.

Odd protuberances

Often a projection or lump will prevent a stone from being seated firmly in the wall. While this can be overcome by

Fig 27 Striking off a protuberance

chinking (*See* Chapter 3), it is far better to remove the projection itself. This is done by striking it sharply with the hammer on its steepest side (Fig 27) and in the direction of the grain, then cleaning up with a bolster. Where such irregularities occur on the face of the stone, they should be removed by striking from the outside towards the centre of the face, and not vice versa, working right round the stone if necessary. Always remember to clean up your stone before you bed it into the wall; attempting to hammer off lumps later can dislodge the mortared stone and crack the wall.

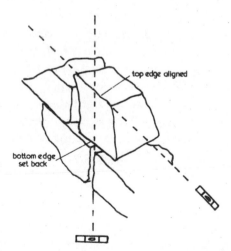

Fig 28 Aligning into the wall a stone with a sloping face

Shaping the face

In the case of random stone, the desired face may not form a perfect right angle with the plane of bedding in the wall (Fig 28). If the angle change is only slight, it can be ignored, providing you bed the stone with the *overlap* to the top making a clean true edge with the facework above (Fig 28) and beneath it. Alternatively, the top edge may be allowed to overlap the wall and, when you come to the next course, do not place the stone above flush with the overhang but inset it to follow the line of the rest of the stones in the face. On no account build to the edges of both top and bottom. Where the angle is pronounced, it should be roughly trimmed by setting the stone on an even surface and nibbling away the overlap as required, working always towards the centre of the stone.

Breaking large pieces

Big chunks of rock must be cut down before they can be used effectively in a wall. Simply to pound away at the rock with the sledgehammer will give you only a heap of small unusable pieces rather than the original big one. Reduce the rock in stages to good building sizes just as you would saw and split a round of tree-trunk into useful logs.

Again, work along the grain with the mason's sledge and wedges to split off large sheets of the desired thickness – obviously these will be thicker than paving slabs – then, with these firmly bedded in the sand box, split them lengthways again by working along a line at right angles to the first in a similar fashion to produce long strips. These can then be broken into the required lengths by resting them at an angle on the edge of the box and striking the centre with the club hammer or sledge. Sharp overhangs and the like can be cleaned off as described above.

Making quoins

Wherever possible, select quoins from your pile of stone at the start, and avoid this cutting work later. If you are lucky enough to obtain demolition stone, there will be plenty of sawn right angles with the delivery, so do not waste them in the body of the wall.

To cut quoins you require a lump hammer, a mason's or pitching chisel, and plenty of patience. Start off with thinnish regular stone and work up to the bigger chunks. It is also best to begin with pieces that are almost right-angled and get the feel of the work by improving these first.

Break off excessive waste lumps simply by nibbling away at the stone with the lump hammer, then fine up to a previously scored mark with the chisel, cutting away a little at a time. Always work round the stone from the outside to the centre angling the chisel slightly into the body of the stone (Fig 29).

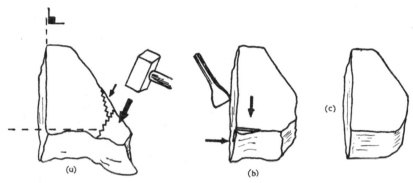

Fig 29 Cutting a quoin (a) rough shaping (b) cutting the angle (c) the finished quoin

Do not try to pitch down very hard stone at the beginning – use the softer limestones. Nothing encourages effort like success. Do not be too upset over the odd failure: the stone may not be an ideal quoin but it will possibly be the exact piece you were looking for in some other spot.

Special angles (*See* Chapter 6. Ends and Openings)

Moving and Lifting Stone

Stone is hard, often awkwardly shaped, rough to the touch, and invariably heavy. Reliance upon pure muscle to move it is often less satisfactory than employing a little science; a five-minute heroic effort at the beginning of the day may cost you two hours of constructive work at the end. Huge rocks that have been delivered should be broken up at the pile and then moved, not moved to the wall first. Never attempt to place a stone on a wall that is too heavy to lower gently into place. Dropping a huge rock into your wall then wriggling it into position will only damage the work you have already completed beneath it. Use very large awkward stones as upright ties in the footings, where they can be rolled or dragged into place and then worked true without disturbing any other work. Never attempt to fit a large stone into a space; build to the large stones with smaller ones.

Many books recommend the construction of 'stone boats' rollers, and bogies for moving stone. Unless you are actually going into the quarrying business these are totally unnecessary. If you need such devices to move the rock, you are not going to be able to build with it unless it is broken up. So break it up first and then move the usable stone.

Occasionally, when digging out footings and foundations, large obstructing rocks are encountered that cannot be utilised *in situ* as part of the wall, or which interfere with levels when paving. These have to be removed, and a few hints on doing so may prevent strains and accidents.

Dig well round the stone first so that you can ascertain its shape and size, but leave a good hard shoulder of soil on one side to act as a fulcrum for levering. Dig deep enough to be able to slip a bar firmly beneath the rock from one side (Fig 30a) and lever the rock loose by pulling either against the side of the trench or against a brick if the soil crumbles. Lever the rock high enough to slip a brick beneath it on each side of the bar. Repeat the process on the other side until the rock is raised clear of its bed on the bricks. Slip a stout plank under one side of the rock (two if the rock is very large), and with the bar begin to 'work' the rock up the planks (Fig 30b). When it is firmly supported on the plank or planks, the latter can be used as levers to raise the rock to ground level and, if the bar is slipped over the hole beneath them, it will act as a temporary roller to haul the rock clear (Fig 30c).

Huge interestingly shaped rocks can be erected as special features in a garden, and the bar-and-plank principle can be used to move and re-site them. Inch large rocks forward with the bar little by little, working each end alternately. Ensure that

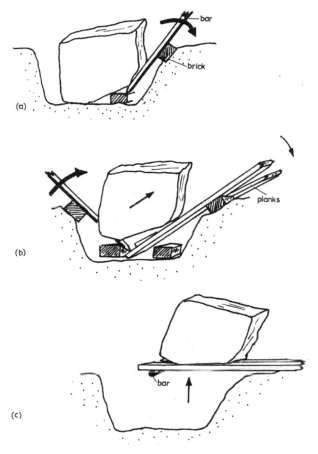

Fig 30 Stages in levering out a large rock

they are orientated with the flattest most stable surface on the ground. Work them up a ramp made of planks, supported underneath, if you need to change levels. Lastly, bed them well into the ground in their chosen site, so that they cannot topple over and injure someone later.

Introduction

Part I has largely concentrated on the basic techniques of working with stone and avoided considerations of the actual constructions themselves. In Part II specific features of building will be examined, utilising the basic techniques already outlined. This is *not* a comprehensive account of what features may be built out of random stone, nor of ideas and instructions for making specific complex structures. It is rather a general guide on how to approach and cope with certain aspects of general construction, thus providing a fuller overall picture for the DIY person attempting to work with stone in home or garden.

Any complex construction is generally based on only a few different but basic methods combined to produce the desired form. For instance, pillars, gateways, windows, and doors all involve the need to turn a right angle in the stonework and are only variations on simple means of tackling ends and openings. Similarly, the fundamental techniques of dealing with curves, steps, bridges, and so on lend themselves to a variety of adaptations, Once such primary methods become familiar, there is no reason why the DIY man or woman should not be able both to design and to build any complex structure out of random stone – from a garden barbecue to a collection of outbuildings.

6 Ends and Openings

Finishing the Wall

Part I discussed various types of finish to a straight run of walling in the form of copings and the like, but made no mention of how to end the wall. Obviously, the wall has to stop somewhere and the end must not only be sound but also in character with the rest of the wall. Alternatively, when building a boundary wall, one might wish to turn the wall through a right angle (90°) to follow that boundary (Fig 31a). All such techniques involving a 'return' (turning the facework through an angle, usually of 90°), whether to make a doorway, gateway, or window, to construct a pillar or follow a boundary, involve the same basic building methods and materials.

Turning through a right angle

The basic building unit for turning through a right angle is the quoin stone. Quoin stones should have been placed in a separate pile (*See* Chapter 2) right from the start so that they are easily accessible when needed. The right-angled face of the individual quoins make up the right-angled return of the total construction. With random stonework, the quoins need not be perfect right angles, providing the overall finished effect of the return is upright and right-angled. Often very attractive and natural-looking returns may be produced from a few well-placed true quoins and many less perfect ones (Plate 4). But do not ruin a good job by building the returns out of artificial stone or – even worse – with concrete blocks. These will always look exactly what they are and will be a permanent reminder that you lacked either the patience or the skill to do the job properly. If you have no quoin stones at all, there other types of finish that can be employed (*See* Chapter 7) without resorting to artificial materials.

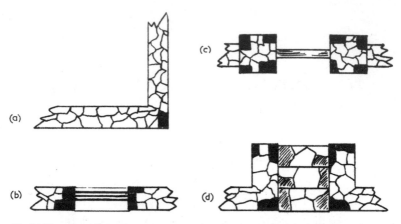

Fig 31 Turning through right angles (angles shaded) (a) walls (b) windows and doors (c) pilasters and gateways (d) steps

Not only must the corner be upright but the stones forming the return must tie back into each face of the body of the wall as well as across the wall. This probably sounds more complicated than it really is, and is best explained by the figures following. All the time, though, you should be thinking in spatial (or three-dimensional) terms rather than considering each plane separately. The ties are most important because rifts must be avoided at all costs, since the ends of the walls usually experience the greatest mechanical battering and must also withstand expansion effects transmitted throughout the main body of the wall. In choosing your quoins, therefore, avoid selecting those of the same size and thickness; randomise them as with the walling stone itself and be sure to include long, thin, flat stones for ties.

To ensure an upright corner a framework can easily be constructed out of battens, and each quoin stone set to touch the upright batten. Personally, I find this method unsatisfactory and prefer to build by eye, checking often with the spirit level. The ability to work in this way comes with experience, however. Remember to stand well back to judge the construction critically as it progresses – but, if working on trestles or scaffolding, beware! A simpler guide can be produced by crossing two building lines at right angles at the corner and sliding these up vertical poles as the building rises.

The footings for the return must be good and deep and perfectly aligned before starting to build. It is good practice to place one long tie-stone in these footings extending deep into one of the faces of the wall (Fig 32a). Build on this for a while, and then place another tie to extend well into the other face of the wall (Fig 32b). If these ties have been judged well, an upright quoin can be set immediately on the long tie and thus maintain the patterned type of building to a big stone discussed earlier (Fig 32c).

(a)

Fig 32 Stages in turning a wall face through a right angle (tie-stones are shaded)

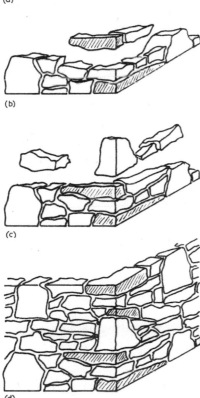

(b)

(c)

(d)

Wherever possible use the long narrow ties to cover as many joints in the stonework beneath as possible, and alternate these ties so that their longest faces extend into different faces of the wall (Fig 32c). Do not allow one joint to lie directly above or very close to a joint beneath, nor attempt to build the corner separate from the rest of the wall, and fill in the gap afterwards. Maintain the continuity of building and the constructional integrity of the whole right through the return. The result will be both more pleasing to the eye and longer lasting.

Avoid topping off with an upright stone that is likely to be knocked loose in time. Instead, finish with a large flattish stone that has fairly long faces on each side of the right angle (Fig 32d). If the body of the wall has a raised coping, then this must continue through the return as well. Choose a solid upright quoin with a flat base and set it directly above the wall angle. Where the copings along the wall vary in size, this corner coping should be one of the largest stones – otherwise the wall will appear to dip at this point.

So far we have considered only the outside face of the wall. Where this turns through an angle of 90°, the stonework on the inside face correspindingly moves through an angle of 270° (Fig 31a). Dealing with this problem (in this instance) is far less complicated than it sounds and only two simple rules need to be observed. Firstly, overlap the stones from each face as much as possible so that the inside faces are tied together. Secondly, ensure the angle remains perfectly vertical and does not drift along one face or the other as you overlap the stones. Quoins are unnecessary on this inside face and stones with good flat faces will answer the problem.

Ending the wall

The procedure for ending the wall – providing it is not to be finished with some other type of construction – is similar. This time two angles of 90° have to be dealt with at the same time, and the end of the wall becomes a third face (Fig 33a). It is essential that this end face be treated in the same fashion as the others: it must be well tied across and on no account should the two corners be built separately and the gaps between merely

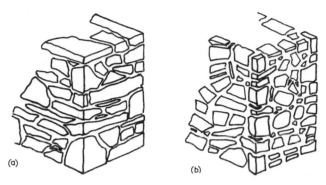

Fig 33 Ending walls (a) good end well tied (b) bad end not tied since quoin stones are all small and even

filled in with any old stone (Fig 33b). If possible, try to obtain two quoin stones with double right angles, fit them exactly right across the end of the wall building them in at different heights; then tie the whole together. Alternatively, a long stone with a single quoin face may be used to extend well across the end, and the remaining small gap cladded with another piece of quoin (Fig 33a).

The greatest problem with wall ends generally occurs when the wall has been built too narrow from the start, and the quoins you have saved are too large to construct a satisfactory end face. In such situations it is best to use a pilaster type of finish (*See* Pillars and Pilasters).

Special angles

Sometimes walls have to be built or corners turned where the change of direction is not a right angle. This is particularly common with boundary-wall gateways that open on to a public highway. Local Authority Regulations may require a particular type of construction (Fig 34) in the interests of safety, and the gateway must be set back from the road, while the walling from gate to boundary flares out at an angle of 45°. This will produce awkward angles of 135° on the face where the wall changes direction, and similar angles of 45° and 135° where the wall joins any pilaster to support the gate (Fig 34).

With random stonework there is little need to go to the trouble of cutting these angles accurately. The wall is effectively

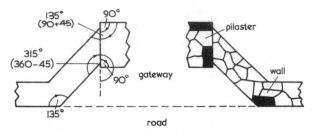

Fig 34 Complex angles produced with flared entrances

'slotted into' the pilaster and the shape of the individual stones is therefore relatively unimportant. (This point is discussed later.) For the exposed 135° angle – and any other angle for that matter – there are ways of solving the problem which, if combined, will certainly allow you to complete the work with the stone available.

Make a firm template of the required angle out of three pieces of batten (Fig 35a). Using this as a guide, sort through your pile of stone, putting to one side any with an angle on the face which approximates to that of the template (Fig 35b). Also put to one

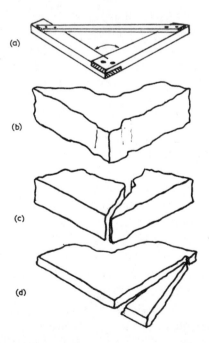

Fig 35 Obtaining stone for special angles (a) template (b) approximate angle (c) using two stones to form the angle (d) cutting the angle

side stones that end in a point at one side of the face (Fig 35c). Finally, select broken pieces of thin stone that can be shaped roughly with ease and trim these to the required angle (Fig 35d).

Use these selected stones to construct the angle. Do not aim to achieve a perfect face on each side, but keep the top of the angle straight and perfectly upright all the time. Do not compromise on this edge but take up the irregularities of dips and bumps in the face of the walls on either side instead. Be sure to tie across the angle with the best shaped stones, particularly where two stones have been used to form the angle. For additional strength the walls can be tied together across the back of the corner when infilling between the faces.

Pilasters and Pillars

Most people have probably never heard of the word 'pilaster' but believe they know exactly what a 'pillar' is. In fact, much of the time they would be calling a pilaster a pillar, for example, a gate-post at the end of a wall. A *pilaster* is a column, generally rectangular in cross-section, fastened to some other structure such as a wall; a *pillar* is a free-standing column of any cross-sectional shape which is slender in relation to its height and supports some overhead structure. Thus the two perform quite different functions and are of different construction.

Pilasters

Before embarking on the actual construction of a pilaster it is worth considering a number of general points which, though important, are often taken for granted.

Most bricklayers build their ends first, and then erect the body of the wall between them. There are many reasons (in their case) for this, the most important probably being that the materials they use are of exact proportions and therefore the constructions can be rigidly drawn up and *exactly* followed. With random natural stonework greater flexibility is possible – especially in the garden – and by experience I have found it best to build the body of the wall first and finish off by tying in the pilasters last of all. This approach allows total flexibility. If you wish to shorten or lengthen the wall you may do so, particularly if you wish to change the position of a gateway; but, more important, you can alter the finished height of the wall as you wish.

Fig 36 Two types of pilaster

Ideally the pilaster should stand no more than one third of the height of the wall above the wall itself (Fig 36), otherwise it looks disproportionately large. If the wall is built first, the most attractive height of the pilaster can then be judged in relation to the wall. Whichever approach is adopted, it is essential to integrate the pilaster with the wall, not simply 'tack it on' or 'hang' a wall between two pilasters. In a very short time the wall and pilaster will part company.

If the wall is of a good thickness a pleasing pilaster effect can be produced. The wall is ended as described previously, but at the topping-off stage is continued upwards in a block at the end until the desired height of the pilaster has been reached (Fig 36a). To produce a square pilaster, a distance equal to the wall thickness is measured along the wall from the end, and two quoins set on the topped-off wall. The pilaster is then built on top of the end of the wall by building through four angles of 90° (as described for pillars later). For a rectangular, chunkier effect the wall thickness may be exceeded by setting the quoins farther back along the wall, but construction still proceeds as for pillars. It is not recommended that the pilaster be narrower than the wall thickness because this would give the impression of a very fragile structure.

If the wall is a little on the narrow side, or you require the more solid effect of the true pilaster (Fig 36b), construction is more difficult, and in fact provides one of the most challenging of the basic techniques in simple stonework. Here one must consider building through four right angles for the four corners of the pilaster, and also two angles of 270° each where the pilaster joins the wall, in addition to keeping the construction square and upright (Fig 36b). Since I have dealt in detail with building through right angles, and four such angles are not four times the problem, but rather the same problem four times, I shall now assume familiarity with the technique. The face at an angle of 270°, however, is new and very often ignored, even though it commonly occurs, so I will consider this in greater detail.

Generally, the right-angled return into the body of the wall will be short, often only a few inches, and it is a great

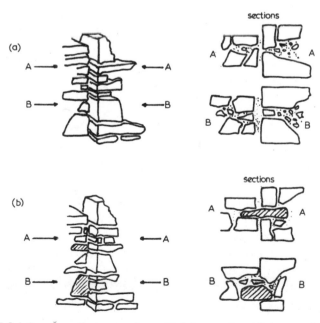

Fig 37 Joining the pilaster to the wall (a) poor insertion – no tie-stones therefore the pilaster is held to the wall solely by mortar (b) good insertion – the wall and pilaster are tied (shaded stones)

temptation to build the right angle correctly with all the quoin stones extending well beyond this distance. The result will be that shown in Figure 37a, and where the pilaster joins the wall a continuous rift of mortar will extend from top to bottom. If you have done this on one side you are likely to have repeated the fault on the other, and the pilaster will then not be tied into the face of the wall at all. It will eventually fall away – particularly if a gate is to be hung on it. It is essential to tie in the pilaster and, since this is not easily done on the face all the way up, in a few places at least long tie stones must extend from the wall into the pilaster and from the wall cavity into the pilaster (Fig 37b).

Topping-off and copings on the pilaster should match the rest of the wall, and four matched quoin stones on edge must be retained for each pilaster if a raised type of coping has been used (Fig 36a). As with the wall ends, these should be at least as large as the largest of the copings along the top of the wall; smaller copings may be used with effect between them (for Figures illustrating this, *see* Chapter 3).

Pillars

For the man or woman who has never attempted any stonework before I do not recommend starting with a pillar. On the other hand, by the time experience has been gained with building a wall and returns, there is no reason at all why a pillar should not then be attempted. One of my early disasters was a pillar built in my own cottage. Largely because of my ignorance of some very important rules – and the absence of any book to help me – the result was a bowed and twisted pillar that simply did not look square at all. It long stood as a reminder and a check to my desire to rush headlong into new, more complicated designs.

So, first the rules. Never try to build a narrow pillar out of random natural stone; with a diameter of less than about 60cm (24in) you will create immense problems for yourself. If circumstances dictate a narrower pillar get the stone cut and dressed to suit before you start. Never try to build a pillar without an adequate supply of quoins. A shed has four right-angled corners and so does each pillar but, whereas a few poor quoins in different walls of the shed are not all that important, they all come together in a pillar. So think in terms of all your stone needing to be quoin stone when working out quantities for pillars. A pillar has a relatively narrow cross-sectional area in relation to its volume and, furthermore, supports some other structure above. The pressure of this small area upon the ground is therefore tremendous and special attention must be paid to the foundations. Finally, pillars can only grow slowly; if you build too high and infill all at once they will slump – patience is essential.

Solid concrete foundations must be built well below ground-level to support the pillar; and to help spread the load they support, their area should exceed that of the pillar itself by a good margin. Such a foundation is sometimes termed a *raft* and a small increase in dimensions considerably extends the area and, consequently, spreads the load satisfactorily. The following example illustrates this. Suppose you require a pillar 60 x 60cm (24in sq), if the foundations are constructed to exceed these dimensions merely by a quarter all round – that is, by 15cm (6in) – the resultant raft will measure 90 x 90cm (30in sq). Consider the cross-sectional area of the pillar at 3,600cm² (4sq ft) compared with the raft area of 8,100cm² (9sq ft). For even with this relatively slight increase in dimensions the area is more than doubled, and thus the load at any point is more than halved. Such a pillar-area/raft-area ratio is quite adequate in ordinary circumstances, although where the ground is exceptionally soft the raft may have to be made even larger. In all cases the pillar should be centred on the raft. This distributes the load more evenly and, because the raft is well below ground-level, it in no way interferes with the above-ground work.

As with walling, the footing course of the pillar should also be below ground-level, and the raft should, therefore, be hardened and finished to a true level before building commences. The building procedure is simply that of turning through four right angles with the quoins, but you should always remember that each face must be well tied-in to the others. The easiest way to do this is to work the tie quoins in a spiral manner around the pillar as it grows. This will ensure that the temptation to work on each face separately is avoided and, as in the case of the pilaster, the whole pillar will be tied throughout its height.

The maximum growth-rate of a single pillar should not exceed more than a metre (3ft) a day unless framework is used. Infilling will tend to push the faces outwards and 'belly' the pillar, but if the infilling is left until later it will form a separate core not tied-in to the faces. In either case the resulting pillar will be weak. It is far better to build several pillars at the same time, each one growing a little, than to attempt to build a single pillar at each session.

How do you keep your pillar perfectly upright, with all corners square? This is perhaps the major worry of everybody who attempts to build a pillar for the first time. Unfortunately, the first time you may not succeed, unless you are a very careful and patient person. There are, however, some aids that may assist the novice. I do not whole-heartedly recommend them since I think it is important to teach the eye to be the most cirtical judge of what is right.

Pillars can be built in a box frame. This means that you construct a rectangular or square box of stout wood about 45cm (18in) high and to the required pillar size (internal box dimensions) and build your pillar within the box. This ensures that the corners are square as you build. The single box frame may be raised on props as the pillar grows (Fig 38) or, alternatively, a series of frames can be built, all being removed by unscrewing one side of each box when the work is completed. To ensure that the box is correctly centred, a length of angle iron or an iron rod is set into the raft foundation from the start in a perfectly perpendicular position and all measurements taken from it (Fig 38). I object to this method of construction on the grounds that you cannot see the facework as the building progresses, nor can you clean the stone or cut out the joints before the mortar has hardened. When the work is finished, only the faces are exposed and, however straight and true, their perfection cannot compensate entirely for messy smeared stonework, poor faces, untidy joints, and ill-chosen stone.

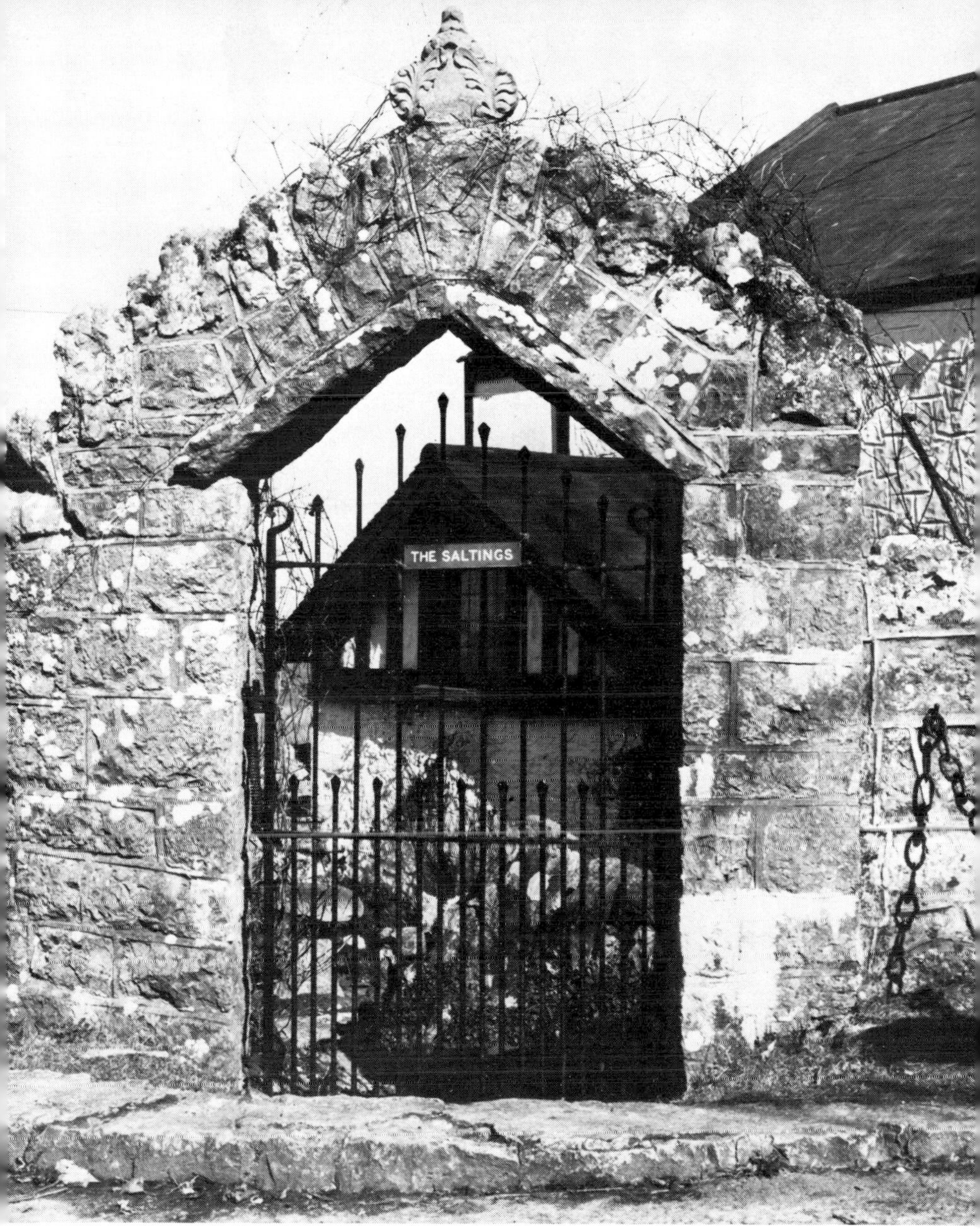

Plate 8 An old peaked arch with double lintel construction

Plate 9 A barbecue area

Plate 10 The cooking area

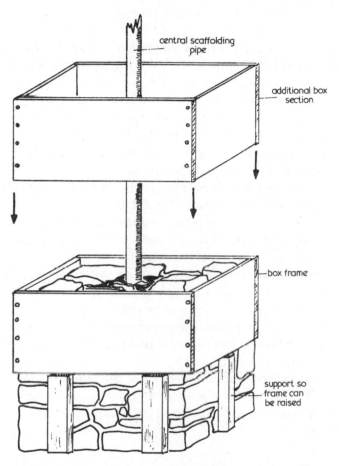

Fig 38 Method of using box construction to produce a pillar

With a little familiarity, a guide for one upright face will enable you to keep the other three faces upright and exact also. Here, a single upright wooden batten set firmly into the ground against one pillar face – and checked regularly with the spirit level – will provide a guide from which you can work. Another batten, marked with the pillar dimensions, can be used against this to maintain the correct size and perpendicularity of the other faces. With this method the facework can be judged as well as cleaned as it progresses.

Pillars generally (technically, always) support some overhead structure, be it balcony, pergola, or lintel. It is therefore essential that pillars which may be spaced far apart are either of equal height or, if on sloping ground, finish at the same horizontal height. Attempting to achieve this is a very sobering lesson on the use of the spirit level. If the bubble in the level is not perfectly centred between the guide-lines, an error of a fraction of a centimetre over the length of a metre rule becomes very significant over ten metres, and painfully obvious to the eye over even greater distances.

One pillar must first be finished to the desired height and all the others levelled off to that pillar. The easiest way to achieve this is to complete the first pillar and then the others to within about 25cm of the judged height and let them set. A stout true timber, such as a rafter, is then laid between the completed pillar and the next incomplete one. With the level centred over this rafter, the end of the unfinished pillar is raised on bricks, and, finally, on pieces of thin slate until the bubble is *exactly* centred. The second pillar is then completed to the level of the rafter. The process is continued down the line of pillars, each being completed in turn.

The tops of the pillars are now all at the required level, and lintels or beams can be placed between them and a new final course of stonework added to bring the pillars up to the top level of these.

Gateways

Gates are generally hung on to the ends of walls or on to pilasters; hence the reason for including them in this chapter. For constructional purposes a gateway can be regarded simply as a gap between two walls. However, if a gate *is* to be hung in the gap, this must be borne in mind from the start. Any gate exerts a great pull upon the wall or pilaster on which it is hung and also upon the fitments (hangers) that fasten it to the wall. Thus, not only must the pilaster be firmly tied to the rest of the wall but also the hangers must be firmly bedded and form an integral part of the pilaster. For this purpose, special masonry hangers with matched hinges are manufactured and should always be used with walling work (Fig 39). A block of wood

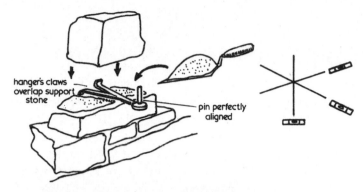

Fig 39 Setting the masonry gate hanger in place

banged into the wall on to which an ordinary hinge is screwed is not a satisfactory substitute.

Generally, a gate should be centred on the pilaster, which allows for firmer bedding of the hangers. Sometimes, however, gates are required to swing back in a particular manner, and the hangers will need to be off-centred for this. In such cases permanence may need to give way slightly to convenience.

Having built many gateways and hung many gates, I can offer one piece of advice from which experience taught me never to deviate. It is much simpler to obtain the gate *before* you start to build the gateway – don't attempt to purchase a gate for the gap. If the gap is already there, build a gate yourself to fit it exactly. Many a contractor has been persuaded to start the pilasters for a customer before the gate arrives and has satisfied neither the customer nor himself.

Once you have the gate with the required hinges attached, and the matching masonry hangers to hand, begin first, by building the pilaster on which the gate is to hang. The first hanger must lie on a narrow flattish stone a few centimetres above the height of the lower gate hinge when the gate rests on the ground alongside it. For this reason you must bear in mind this position from the footings up – otherwise the hanger will be positioned too high or too low, depending on the stone thickness you have available. The hanger is bedded in mortar on this stone so that it is not only centred but is also horizontal and the hanger pin is vertical (Fig 39). A large stone is then bedded across the claw of the hanger and the hanger again checked to ensure that it remains true. Continue to build up the pilaster as described, stopping work just short of the approximate position of the upper hanger. Leave the mortar and lower hanger to harden off and set firm before continuing.

The rest of the work is determined once the lower hanger is firmly in position, and thus it is essential that it be 'set true' from the start. The lower hinge of the gate is then slipped over the pin and the gate made horizontal by supporting it on blocks, and then vertically centred by means of battens (Fig 40a). Ensure that the gate is firmly wedged, then judge the correct position of the upper hanger and its supporting stone in the wall. The hanger should then be removed, the pilaster built to the required level, and the hanger replaced and bedded as with the lower hanger. With the gate firmly in position and the hanger replaced and bedded in the stonework (not merely propped in by the hinge), the remainder of the stonework may be finished and allowed to set.

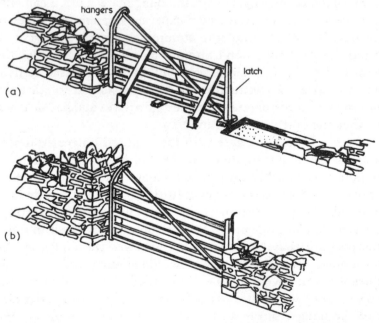

Fig 40 Stages in building pilasters and hanging gate together

When set, the props for the gate are removed and the gate should be perfectly hung. The second pilaster can quickly be built by using the vertical side of the hanging gate as guide, and the latch slot or furniture correctly positioned with reference to the gate itself (Fig 40b). Waiting for the mortar to harden takes time, but that should not worry the DIY worker, who is far more likely to produce a well-hung gate matched to the wall by this method.

Common faults occur if you try to fit the gate to the pilasters at a later stage: the gap is either too large or too small; the hangers are not perfectly in line or not the correct distance apart for the hinges; or the latch housing is incorrectly positioned. This may not be the fault of the stoneworker but due to very slight variations in the actual gate measurement compared with those ordered. All such problems are equally aggravating and generally result either in the demolition of one or both pilasters, or the rebedding of the hangers, a far less satisfactory solution. So, do not start without the gate and do work with patience.

Doors and Windows

Undoubtedly, examination of the building of doorways and windows belongs to this chapter on Ends and Openings, but certain other considerations make their inclusion at all more of a problem. Both doors and windows are generally associated with dwellings, and as such are subject to building regulations. Furthermore, any person's home is probably the most expensive single item he or she will ever purchase and will also be the most valued. By giving scant treatment to such major features as doors and windows, which may also be part of the supporting structure of the house, I could be guilty of persuading the DIY man to undertake work that I am unable to describe in adequate detail within the scope of this book. When the reader has already had building experience, the earlier coverage of returns and gateways, together with his own knowledge, is probably sufficient to enable him to work with stone on such structures. But for the DIY beginner I prefer to offer no advice – rather than mere scanty assistance – as far as building new structures that incorporate windows and doors is concerned.

For some of you, however, especially those with old stone cottages and houses, advice on simple tidying and replacement might be appreciated and therefore I have dealt with the problems involved in the chapter on Demolition and Renovation (Chapter 10). Both there and in Chapter 8, features such as the placement of lintels, the construction of arches and the like are considered in relation to particular problems rather than in a constructional manner.

7   Circles and Curves

Until now we have been talking of structures out of random stone that follow rigidly straight lines, true levels, and well-defined angles. When dealing with curves, slopes, circles, and flowing lines through changing levels, the basic tools for laying out and finishing the work do not assist as much as they do in the case of more formal structures. The craftsman's eye and judgement become all-important, often completely replacing the artificial aids, the aim being to work on what pleases the eye rather than depending on the dictates of a bubble in a spirit level. Thus the approach to 'flowing' work in stone is rather different from that described before, although the basic constructional techniques remain the same.

Broadly speaking, this approach is that of the landscape-gardener, although curving structures are not out of place inside the home, as will be shown later. It is also that of the artist and designer rather than the artisan. Thus, personal views are expressed far more freely in this type of work, and many who wish to use stone in this manner will quickly adopt their own styles – which may well differ from mine.

Circles

Raised beds
With perfectly circular designs a builder's line may be used as an aid to set out the work. Hammer an iron bar firmly into the ground at the centre of the proposed circle; make a large loop at one end of the line so that it slides easily around the bar; and then slip it over the bar. Knot the other end of the line tightly round a cold chisel or line pin at the required radius of the circle and scribe the outer limit of the design (Fig 41a) until a perfect circle is produced. If you find you are not getting a perfect circle, check that the line is not snagging or winding itself up

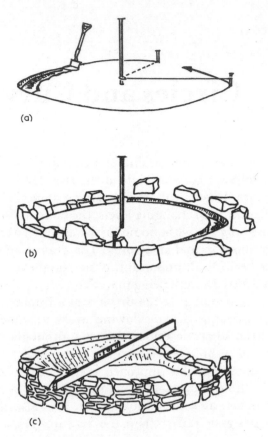

(a)

(b)

(c)

Fig 41 Stages in building raised circular beds

around the bar, and be sure to keep the chisel or pin·upright.

With a spade, deeply mark the circle all round first, then dig out a footing trench for the wall to the inside of this mark. On sloping ground the bottom of the trench should be dug more deeply on the higher side, then trued up with the footing mix. Since raised beds are not usually very high, concrete foundations for the walls are rarely necessary. Building the wall follows the same procedures as described in Chapter 3. The same rules apply: build to big stones, overlap the joints, and so on. With a raised bed, however, you will be building only one face like a retaining wall, so it must be backed well with rubble and mortar as you progress (Fig 41c). Note that with circular constructions it is possible for two upright stones to come together when the two arms of the wall meet if spacing is rigid. Therefore it is useful to lay these uprights all round the outside of the footing trench to get the spacing even before mortaring them into their permanent positions in the footings.

Since these walls will generally be fairly low, the topping-off stage must be borne in mind from the start. As far as possible, try to place the last course of uprights to the finished level, checking round and across the wall all the time with the spirit level on a batten (Fig 41c). Try to avoid topping off with thin stones, and especially a series of thin stones. These will certainly become dislodged in time as the flower beds are worked. Similarly, never place upright copings round a raised bed – these are not only easy to dislodge when digging but also make weeding very difficult.

Wall height is extremely important and, generally, the smaller the circle the lower the wall should be, otherwise a turret effect will be produced. As a rough guide, the wall should never be higher than about one-third of the radius of the bed. So a bed 2m (approx 2yd) across would have a wall of about 30cm (1ft) high. Where turret effects are required, these will generally be associated with other walls or steps and thus they are also pilasters. As such they are discussed again later.

Fig 42 Constructing a paved circle – from the outside. Note the triangular shape of the outer stones

Paved circles

For paving circles proceed to draw out the design as described above then dig out the whole of the interior of the design, levelling off on uneven ground. Pave from the perimeter of the circle inwards, apart from a gap for access, using spirit level and long batten across the circle to maintain the levels. For the outside of the circle, triangular or trapezoidal shapes of random paving should be selected with their bases touching each other on the perimeter (Fig 42). This will ensure a clean outer edge with few or no gaps.

If circles of paving stone of a contrasting material are required within a general body of paving, I have found it best to leave these circles until last. Simply mark them out and complete the main paving, leaving the circles as ground-level beds initially. This will allow you an opportunity to change your mind if you are not satisfied with the design. Furthermore, it is easier to maintain the level across the circle and avoid the stones standing proud on one side.

Combinations of walling and paving

In many garden designs it is pleasing to use raised, curved, and circular beds to break up areas of paving. It is important always to construct and complete the walling and any other jobs prior to starting the paving. Not only is it far easier to fit the paving to the raised walls, but the paving does not get stained or damaged by the process of walling.

Circular designs may also be linked together attractively but a few design rules should be noted. Never make the circles of equal area – vary the size. Even a small change in diameter adds to the final appearance. If more than two linked circles are required, ensure that the centres of the circles do not lie on a straight line but themselves form part of a curve. With linked designs, the largest circle should be the complete one and the smaller ones slotted into that. This is particularly important with raised circular beds, where the largest circle should also be the highest.

Sometimes attractive designs may be produced by paving over raised circles – particularly where ponds are incorporated into the garden. In such cases, the topping-off on the wall need not be perfect since the paving will be levelled off over this. It is, however, important to choose the outer ring of paving with care as it must overlap the walling by an inch or so, must touch at the perimeter as far as possible, yet must bed well back over the wall. For such work thinner paving material, such as slates and limestone rivings, tend to produce a better effect than thick flagstone chunks.

Pilasters (Plate 5)

In the previous chapter it was mentioned that if insufficient quoin stone was available for building a square or rectangular pilaster this could be overcome by using a different type of design. That design is the circular pilaster constructed of random stone, but it must be emphasised that it is not the *simpler* form of construction. To keep the circular pilaster not only upright but also perfectly tubular, while at the same time strongly keying it into a wall and maybe also supporting a gate, is probably one of the most difficult of all tasks in random stonework.

Because of the random nature of the building material, it is impossible to build slender circular pilasters. They must be bold and chunky; therefore try to match the character of any walling to this chunky effect from the very start. The smaller the diameter, the greater the problems, so circular pilasters are rarely built less than 75cm (30in) in diameter – and bigger than this if at all possible.

The problems are due to the rapidly decreasing perimeter of the circle as one approaches the centre of the pilaster. Figure 43 illustrates this with a pilaster of 100cm (3ft) diameter. The outside perimeter will be approximately 315cm (10ft), but if the average size of the stone available is 25cm (10in), the inside perimeter will be halved to 157cm (5ft). It is fairly obvious, therefore, that if rectanguilar blocks of stone are used for building, even though their inside ends fit closely together, the outside perimeter of the pilaster (the face) will be half mortar. This has to be overcome by selecting wedge-shaped blocks that taper back from the face into the body of the pilaster. This necessity, in turn, creates further problems of strength within the pilaster. All the forces are directed downwards and outwards from the centre of the pilaster and tend to act to push out the facing stones where they are weakest – rather like pushing out a wedge instead of hammering it in tighter (Fig 43c). Thus, tying in the faces of the walling is difficult but

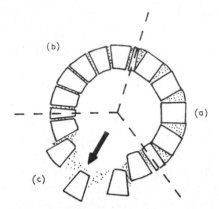

Fig 43 Problems with round pilasters. Area (a) – regular blocks result in large areas of mortar on the face. Area (b) – shaped blocks give even joints, but natural forces tend to push the stones outwards and apart – area (c)

essential – and so is the special method of infilling the centre described later.

One of the simplest methods of overcoming the problem is to make sure from the start that you have a wide range of stone of various shapes and sizes, including a lot of very small stone. This will enable you to 'cheat' at the awkward places where the gaps are too small or strangely shaped to use an ordinary stone, but too large to fill in comfortably with mortar.

The initial circular shape can be scribed out as discussed earlier, but for the beginner it is probably best to set a short length of scaffold piping permanently in the centre of the pilaster foundations which can be used to maintain the accuracy of construction throughout the work. Good concrete foundations are advisable and these should be set, complete with centre pipe, before actual building commences. Note that the pipe must be perfectly vertical – otherwise, the pilaster will lean to one side. As with all building, the footings must be below ground-level and level themselves. Try to maintain the building-to-a-big-stone technique but ensure that the big stones, especially, taper inwards – otherwise, there will be little room for the stones between. Keep a line loop permanently over the scaffolding pipe and check that the face of each stone is not only perfectly aligned on the perimeter but is also upright. It is essential that no stones slope downwards and outwards.

Long narrow tie-stones – so useful in straight walls – cannot be used without some shaping in circular pilasters. These can be roughly shaped at the ends and backs, as described in

Chapter 5. These ties provide horizontal strength and prevent the development of vertical rifts in the wall, so common when using small stone.

The interior of the pilaster must be completely filled in with concrete as the building progresses, and this bonded well to the face stone. In addition, metal rods or straps can be used at regular intervals across this central cavity to tie the face together.

Never attempt to rush building a circular pilaster. Let it set well after building some 30–50cm (12–18in) before going higher. If you do not do so, the concrete infilling will push out the stone, producing a barrel-shape or – worse still – the whole thing will collapse.

If a gate is to be hung on the pilaster adopt the same approach as for the rectangular structure and be even more patient.

Copings can be used with effect on circular pilasters, particularly upright copings. It is usually better to keep these of roughly equal size with random stonework. The mortar at the top of the pillar should be domed to help shed water to the exterior, and a further large central coping stone may be added.

Turret beds are generally a hybrid between pilasters and raised beds and can be used with great effect on steeply sloping ground to change wall levels sharply without being too noticeable. They are started like the pilaster, with a removable centre bar, and solidly infilled for some two-thirds of their height. The remainder of the building is done as for a circular bed leaving small weepholes for drainage. The centre cavity is then moulded to a shallow dish shape with mortar to the level of the weeps and, when hardened, filled with soil for planting.

Curves

Curved walls in the garden
Looping curves across a rectangular plot can create an illusion of space and distance, and can further produce the excitement of the unusual and the unknown. Similarly, the use of curves in steeply sloping gardens offers a far more imaginative approach

to the boring, but common, division of the area into a series of rigidly defined, discrete terraces. Curves are flexible and allow a flexible approach to landscaping – make the most of them!

With curving walls, the laying-out procedure is at the same time the most difficult and the most critical aspect of the project and must be approached with patience and fortitude. A large number of pointed short battens or stakes are the first prerequisite, and these are hammered into the ground at short intervals along the whole length of the proposed wall. View the stakes from all angles and at various distances as if they were the completed wall moving individual pegs as required to achieve the desired effect. With a long straight batten check a combination of three different pegs at a time, proceeding from one end of the wall to the other. If at any point three pegs lie in a straight line, one peg must be moved and the whole laying-out procedure repeated (Fig 44). Failure to do so will later result in an anomalous straight section that can be quite an eyesore in an overall curved wall.

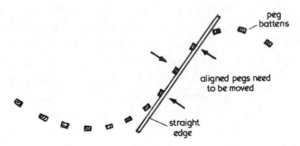

Fig 44 Laying out the curve for a wall

When satisfied with the arrangement of the pegs, use plenty of dry sand to lay out the whole length of the wall shape, and again repeat the procedure adopted above with the pegs until you are certain that the overall shape is a continuously curving single entity. Only then should you dig out the footings trench and set in the footings for the whole length of the wall. If you leave the work partly done and come back to it the following week, the curves will become flattened and the continuity lost.

Once the wall has been laid out satisfactorily and the footings placed, walling may proceed as described in Chapter 3, obeying the same rules and hints. If the wall is retaining a high bank, it is advisable to include some weepholes near the base. If the wall is level, topping-off is only slightly more complicated than with a straight wall, and an adaptation of the builder's-line procedure described in Chapter 3 can be used. With a curved wall, the line cannot be stretched between two level points and run along the top of the wall. Upright stones must therefore be set at the finished level, using the spirit level and batten in positions that tend to divide the wall into a series of straightish lines around the curve (Fig 45). The line is stretched between these sections and, if necessary, curved into deep bellies with a peg, and topping off completed section by section (Fig 45). Where pegs are used to curve the line it is essential to use the eye from a distance to ensure that the batten causes neither dip nor peak where the line touches it. Once the wall is topped off, copings, if required, are straightforward to add.

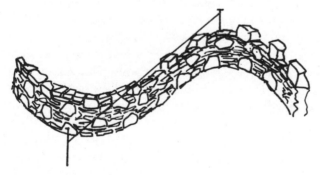

Fig 45 Topping off curved walls in sections

A retaining wall rarely has copings, and if it is built up against a raised lawn it is generally best to grass right over the top of the stonework to facilitate mowing.

Where a sloping wall is required, topping-off is very much more difficult, and sections often need to be taken down and redone – so be warned! The spirit level is of no use, but a large number of pegs and battens are indispensable. I find it makes little difference whether you start to top off from the lower end of the slope and work uphill or vice versa. Do not, however, attempt to work outwards from the middle unless it is unavoidable. This is far more difficult and usually results in two different gradients from the very beginning.

Decide the finished height at one end and mortar in one large upright at this point. Proceeding from here, hammer in the batten pegs along the length of the back of the wall – this is easier if a retaining wall is being built, since shorter pegs can be used at intervals of about 50cm (18in). Progressively hammer these pegs deeper until their tops represent the continuously falling curving line of the final finished height of the wall. To achieve this continuity you must remember to stand back and view the pegs at eye-height as you hammer them down. Often a second person's assistance is invaluable here – you stay back and direct the hammering operations from a distance. If reasonably happy with the peg-level, top off a short section; then view this again from a distance. When you are satisfied that the section accurately follows the peg-level, complete the wall.

This method may seem time-consuming and cumbersome but if it is not observed you are likely to run into all kinds of problems. The greatest danger arises where the gradient is not set out over the whole length of the wall. The person who starts sloping upwards from the bottom end of the wall with no overall gradient guide may end up requiring scaffolding to complete the wall! Even the tiny gradient of 3cm: 1m will double the height of a metre wall over the relatively short distance of 33m.

For topping off slopes, slightly wedge-shaped long stones are a great asset since they can be used to match the gradient without being put in lopsidedly. Try to avoid topping off with a couple of layers of regular rectangular stones aligned along the slope and distinct from the main wall construction.

When dealing with slopes, wherever possible avoid changes of gradient in a continuous run of wall because this will produce the impression of a hump or dip at the change-over point. Try to keep all slopes even, and break changes of slope by means of features such as steps, turret beds, or pilasters.

Plate 11 An integrated terrace

Plate 12 A stone fireplace

Curved pavings

Paving in curves is a lot easier than walling, the laying-out of the curves really being the only extra problem compared with straight-sided paving. Start out with pegs as you would for walls, and emphasise the shape with plenty of sand. Ensure that there are no straight runs within the curve. Do not slope large areas of paving steeply – wet paving stones are extraordinarily slippery. Overcome changes of level by means of linked low walls and steps (Plate 6) and use changing patterns of curves at the different levels. Remember to overlap the walls slightly with the paving to create depth and shadow.

A special form of curved paving is also used in the finish to a garden pool – a detailed account of pool construction is beyond the scope of this present book, but I will add a few hints on the paved surround for concrete pools. The surround is used not only to make a pool attractive but also to define its shape clearly and to determine the level. Remember that you cannot slope water! Therefore the surround to a pool must be perfectly level, although the depth of the pool itself can vary. Overlap the top of the pool with paving; then mortar and waterproof the lip underneath right up to the base of the paving stones themselves. Run the surround of the pool into another feature such as a wall or path, so that the pool is not isolated but forms an integral part of the overall design.

Curved paths have already been discussed in the general paving chapter. Other special forms of curves, such as steps and arches, are dealt with separately in the following chapter (Chapter 8).

8   Steps and Arches

Steps

Before going into the actual building aspects of steps, the DIY stoneworker is well-advised to give thought to their function. A sound understanding of what is expected of any structure, and the use or abuse it will receive, invariably results in a sounder structure itself. We may well ask therefore: what are steps actually for and how do they perform this function?

Basically, steps provide a convenient and permanent means of either ascent or descent between two planes on different levels. In this loose definition, the important words are 'convenient' and 'permanent'. Lifts and ladders can fulfil a similar function but do not satisfy these conditions – nor do ramps, which have to be very steep and dangerous if they are to compete with the compactness of a flight of steps. However, convenience must be judged not solely in terms of the use of the steps themselves but also in the way their presence and location might affect the different levels they connect. Because they are permanent they cannot be hidden away when not in use and there are therefore aesthetic considerations to bear in mind, too. They achieve their function uniquely by converting the normal forward action into both a forward and upward (or downward) motion, and the ease with which they do so is a measure both of their effectiveness and the skill of the person building them. Unfortunately, the perfect set of steps is perfect for one person only, since we all differ in size and manner of walking. Some compromise is therefore inevitable.

Design

The first aspect of design will not be of the steps themselves but of how and where they are to be sited. If they are to lead up to a doorway directly this is no problem. Where there is flexibility of positioning, however, other factors can be taken into account. Remember that steps take up space in three dimensions; they will therefore either jut out on to a lower level or will cut into an upper level, or do a bit of both (Fig 46a and b). Always decide from the outset which type of construction is going to be both the most convenient and the most pleasing. If your steps are to descend from an open grassed area down to a restricted paved terrace, set the steps right back into the grassed area. If the upper area is restricted, leave this clear and run your steps out in the clear lower area. If both areas are restricted, build your steps parallel to the walling instead of at right angles to it, or else restrict them to a position at one end (Fig 46c).

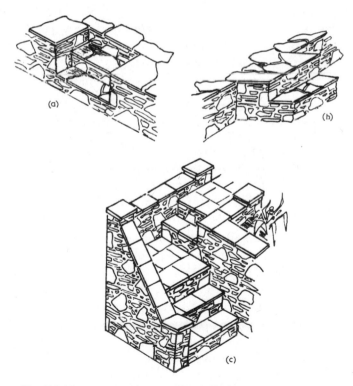

Fig 46 (a) Inset steps (b) protruding steps (c) complex steps

Analyse positioning in relation to usage. Do not site a flight of steps alongside or underneath a rotary clothes-line – this may sound obvious but it is surprising how easily it is done when you have already constructed your path to the line area. Secondly, do not have a flight of steps leading directly down to a huge picture window or a set of glass doors. People and objects often go down steps in a rush without stopping at the bottom. Either move the steps to one side or angle them away from the glass. The same applies if the steps lead out from your property to the road. Where steps lead up to a raised terrace against the house, the steps should not be automatically positioned in the centre because they may break the run of the terrace. Try moving them to one side for a more pleasing effect (*See* Plate 11).

The possible designs for the flight of steps itself are infinite and, indeed, some steps may form the most arresting and dramatic focal point in the architecture of a building. Witness the famous staircases favoured in some of the great houses throughout Britain and Europe, particularly those built during the eighteenth and nineteenth centuries.

Construction Techniques

Digging out

Having decided on position, style, and so on, mark out the rough area of the steps with pegs and string but do not attempt any building until the associated features are almost completed. Retaining walls separating the different levels should be finished, leaving a substantial gap for the steps. The two levels themselves should be raked out to their final heights to provide the starting and finishing points for the steps. Should the levels be altered *after* the steps are constructed the latter will either be uneven or have to be built again. If the steps run into the upper level, considerable digging-out is required, and must be started from *behind* the retaining wall to accommodate the bottom step. The distance you dig back to form a gently sloping ramp is determined by the dimensions of the steps themselves and the difference in height between the two levels. These proportions are discussed later.

Never make the steps narrow with high walls to each side: they will then appear far steeper and more dangerous than they actually are. Thus, when digging out, it is important to allow plenty of room to accommodate each of the side walls. Tend to dig away rather more than you think you really need to and cart this unwanted earth well away before you start building.

Building the side walls

The walling must extend deeper into the ground than the steps themselves, so the footings will need to be set into a trench on each side of the sloping ramp. However, because you are building on a slope these footings themselves must be stepped (*See* Chapter 3), and the footing stones set in horizontal courses. When building at right angles into the upper level, the side walls must be kept perfectly level at the same height. Use the spirit level on a batten across the steps to maintain this topping-off level. Where other types of steps (discussed later) are built, the side walls may slope. If this is the case, either keep the two slopes exactly the same or make them completely different, especially if the steps separate more than two levels (Fig 46). Avoid making the slopes approximately right – they will certainly *look* very wrong! It is generally best if raised copings are avoided along walls bounding steps. People use the walls as banisters, and the copings not only tend to get pulled away but are also rough to the touch.

Building the steps

Each step consists of two parts: the *riser*, which is the vertical face, and the *tread*, which is on the horizontal plane. The riser is built on walling principles, the tread on those of paving. All the risers must be completed before the paving is started. Measurements of the individual steps are important. The maximum height of any riser when completed should be no more than 20cm (8in), the minimum depth of any tread no less than 30cm (12in). Work out the number of steps required in the flight, bearing these figures in mind. Thus, to change to a level 1m higher requires five steps and, because these are each 30cm deep, the flight will extend a minimum of 1½m into the upper

level. The gradient therefore is not 45° but shallower, and the
flight will take up rather more space than one expects. This can
cause problems, particularly in restricted areas. By using
different shapes of flights, however, it is possible to get round
this problem and I will deal with such possibilities later.

Build the first riser in continuation with the retaining wall
and the footings well-bedded. Try to avoid using a single course
of evenly matched stones; instead, select thinner stone and get
two or more courses. The overall topping course should be
level, but slight irregularities with individual stones do not
matter since these will be paved over. The bottom riser should
measure about 20cm *minus* the paving thickness, say 5cm,
giving a riser of about 15cm. All the other stone risers are built to
20cm. This is important if the step heights are to remain even.
When the bottom riser is paved over, the step height is raised by
5cm to 20cm, but the height of the riser above is *reduced* by 5cm.
This reduction is corrected when the latter riser in turn is
paved, and so on to the upper level. If using a patterned
technique in the walls continue it through the risers. Thus, if the
large upright is centred in the first riser, use two off-centred
uprights in the next riser, and alternate this procedure as you
build (Fig 46). Backfill behind the riser with solid rubble and
mortar, so that the steps will not sink with time.

Pave the steps, if you want to finish them in one operation,
from the top down. If you work in the other direction you will be
treading on and disturbing the fresh paving. Pave with a very
slight fall from the back to the lip of each step to shed water and
prevent puddles after rain. This fall must not be pronounced,
for steps get slippery and potentially dangerous when wet. The
centre of the steps get most wear; therefore, where possible, use
the largest pieces of paving in the centre and fit round these
with smaller pieces to the sides. Overlap the risers slightly but
do not use narrow pieces of paving for this; they must bed well
back into the tread – otherwise, they will break loose with wear.

Protruding steps

With protruding steps, side walls may be absent but the
risers themselves have to be returned along the flight of the

steps. These returns will usually be right-angled and therefore quoin stones are required for both the walling and for paving the treads (Fig 46a). As before, complete all the walling prior to starting the treads. In this case, use larger pieces of paving to the *outside* of the treads, since these will be the ones most vulnerable to displacement. Protruding steps, if of more than three risers, should generally run alongside the retaining wall (Fig 46c), not at right angles to it, because this would prevent the marked division of the lower level from the upper and reduce the somewhat overpowering effect of a great jutting mass of stonework.

Curved steps

Where space is restricted, and the change in levels very large, curving and spiral flights of steps not only overcome the space problem but can look very beautiful (Plate 7). Their major drawback is that they are extremely difficult to build. The side walls are of the curving sloping type and all the complexities that this involves must be taken into account prior to building. Furthermore, the curves are tighter, and the working space far more restricted than is normally experienced with flowing garden-wall construction. The techniques, however, remain the same and need not be repeated.

The construction of the risers, on the other hand, varies slightly from that described above for straight steps. In any series of parallel curves, the run of walling to the inside of the curve will be shorter than that on the outside; thus the treads cannot remain perfectly rectangular throughout the curve. The differences in length must be estimated and compensated for by making one side of the steps narrower than the other. Try, however, to keep the centre of each tread roughly 30cm (12in) deep as described above, and no less than 25cm (10in). If the curve is S-shaped, obviously the narrow side of the steps will reverse as the direction of the curve changes. Often it is easier to overcome the problems of keeping an evenly-matched slope on each side of the steps by avoiding them. This can be achieved by means of a turret bed to one side of the steps, and a sloping wall on the other side running down to the new lower level.

Steps to buildings

Steps leading to doorways in houses are generally very low, take a great deal of wear, and may be a focal point. Where possible they should be paved with a single slab of hardwearing stone to avoid eroding the softer mortar and grouting between paved joints. Slates are an excellent material for this and have been used extensively for this purpose since time immemorial. Remember to keep the surface of the steps below door level and to slope it away very slightly from the house.

Where external steps run between levels alongside the building, as with split-level houses, a waterproof membrane should be incorporated in the construction next to the house. This will prevent damp attacking the outer skin of the building. Also, the area at the bottom of the steps should be well drained away from the dwelling to prevent the collection of water here that might eventually damage structural foundations.

Internal stone staircases

In the case of a stone-built house or cottage, internal stone staircases can be very effective, providing one gives the matter a little thought beforehand. Firstly, be certain that the rooms are large enough to take the staircase, since it is a bulky construction and will be overpowering in a restricted space. Do not build a stone staircase against a plastered and painted or papered wall – it must blend back into a similar internal stone wall. Do not attempt to build in a cupboard or alcove beneath the stairs unless you have considerable structural building experience. Run the stairs from an open position up to a corner of the room (unless the room is very large), both to assist construction and for aesthetic reasons. Remember that the staircase will need either a banister, the supporting posts of which must be firmly fixed to the treads, or an enclosing stone panel from floor to ceiling faced on both sides. A metal banister is probably the simplest option and should be made to measure, and fitted, by a competent craftsman.

Stone steps are cold and can be rough to the touch. To reduce discomfort and enhance the beauty, build the treads from single pieces of cut and polished stone. You will have to obtain these from firms specialising in such work, and it is often a good idea to bevel the upper edge of the stone lip very slightly. Such firms will advise you on how the stone should be maintained to preserve the natural finish.

Arches

One of the most challenging and satisfying of all structures to build in natural stone is the arch. Simple arches are supported by pillars, but more usually they are associated with walls and pilasters and they often from part of other structures, such as bridges, gateways, alcoves, and the like. Although they offer great scope for variety in design, basically they can be divided into those that are curved and those that are made up of straight runs of stonework. Most arches require the initial construction of a wooden frame or 'form' both to support the stone and to maintain the symmetry of shape during building.

Straight arches

The term is perhaps something of a misnomer since the very word 'arch' automatically conjures up visions of graceful curves. The lintel, seen over every doorway and window is a straight arch and its construction is examined in detail in Chapter 10.

However, straight arches are not confined to the simple lintel form but may be seen where a peaked effect is desired (Plate 8). The simplest way to build this is by means of a double-lintel construction requiring slabs of massive even stone for the lintels, such as old pavings or sills. These arches must be supported on a framework of timber which is left in place until the mortar has hardened.

To produce the type of construction shown in Plate 8, two slabs of stone of matching proportions are placed in such a way that they lean together at the apex of the arch, while the remainder of the stonework is built over them. First, the supporting walling or pilasters are completed to a height that approximates to the required position of the base of the lintels. The wooden framework is then made up from stout straight timber such as a 4 × 2 rafter to the exact internal dimensions of the whole arch and set firmly in position between the supporting stonework (Fig 47). Each lintel is set in position separately, the edges where they meet having been cut to form a mitred, narrow, vertical joint. At their bases the lintels must be locked behind a firmly set upright stone in the wall, or a pilaster (Figs 47 and 48).

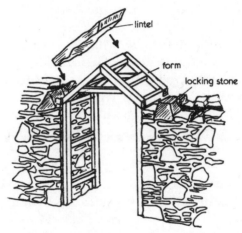

Fig 47 Wooden form in position for construction of double lintel peaked arch

These points are of great importance. Natural loads on the lintels force them downwards and outwards. If, however, the point where they touch is bevelled, the edges of the stone are pressed tighter together the greater the load, thus transmitting the load outwards to the supporting work. If not 'locked' in this way, the downward force opens the joint, causing the arch to collapse at its apex (Fig 48a, b). It is obviously important, therefore, that the supporting stonework be built to accommodate these extra forces. Flimsy, hastily constructed pilasters will be pushed apart by the arch, as will any stonework that has not hardened before the lintels are set in position.

If the lintels cannot be cut at the apex to the required angles, the locking effect may be achieved by the use of a *keystone*

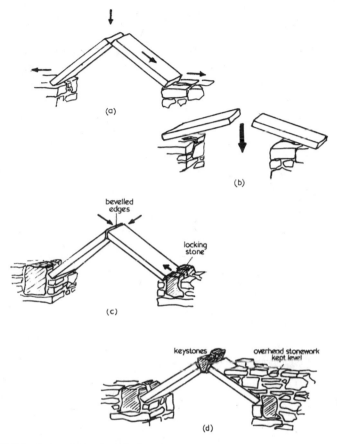

Fig 48 Principles of the double lintel construction (a) incorrect (b) resulting collapse (c) correct – bevelled (d) with keystones in place

between them. This will be trapezium-shaped in section and will have the effect of tightening the joints under load (Fig 48d). With the single horizontal type of lintel construction, the main forces are all downwards, particularly at the centre of the lintel. Thus the use of the peaked or curved arch, though more difficult to build, provides a far superior type of construction, since it redistributes the loads to the supports.

Build the stonework over the lintels working from the supports towards the apex, tying the stonework well back into the supports. Do not slope the stone up the lintels but keep it horizontal as with normal building (Fig 48c). This will provide greater strength as well as a more attractive finish. Copings and decorations are a matter of personal choice. Only when the pillar is finished and set should you remove the timber frame and clean up mortar snubs and so on with the hammer and cold chisel. If you are contemplating a series of such arches the timber framework can be used again and will ensure that all your arches are of identical proportions.

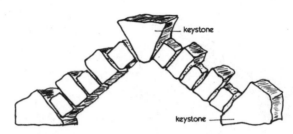

Fig 49 Shaped stone for peaked arch built from separate units

Peaked arches may also be built without using the double-lintel construction. Instead, the supporting arms are made up of selected shaped stones with keystones at the apex and where the arch joins the pilaster (Fig 49). The timber frame used here, though of the same shape, must have cross supports beneath the arch (*See* the next section on curved arches). This may be covered in hardboard or ply, providing a complete supporting area to work on, which facilitates the building but unfortunately prevents you from seeing the under-arch facework and from cleaning out the joints before the mortar has set really hard.

The approximate shapes of the keystones are important and are required for each face of the arch. Their shape and orientation is outlined diagrammatically in Figure 49, and the stone between should be evenly matched and rectangular. Proceed with building as for the double-lintel construction and, with the frame in place, build over the arch evenly from each side, finally setting the centre keystone in place. Stonework above the arch itself should again be built on the horizontal plane and tied well back into the associated walling.

Curved arches

The curved type of arch is not only the most beautiful to look at; it is also – if built correctly – the strongest form of arch construction and a most satisfying achievement for the stoneworker. The choice of stone from a random pile of rocks, and their rough shaping to form the arch, are perhaps the most important primary considerations. If you do not feel up to selecting your arch stones, visit a firm that specialises in sawing and dressing stone, taking an exact template – preferably in wood – of the proposed arch with you. They will then cut the stone to produce a perfect shape and fit, and you will be shown how to 'build by numbers'.

The more determined, those who relish a challenge, and those who believe that their arches should be built of the same random material as the rest of the work, must constantly be on the look-out for evenly matched trapezoidal blocks of the type used in the construction of the round pilaster, but they must be still larger. This time, however, the facework is on the inside of the curve, and the stone should be trimmed with this in mind.

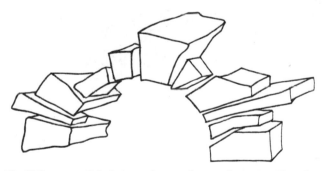

Fig 50 Some useful shapes of stone for random curved arches

As with the straight peaked arch, three shaped keystones are very important and some useful random-stone shapes for arch construction are illustrated in Figure 50. While building the arch, constantly remind yourself that the main thrust is downwards and outwards from the apex to the supports. Build to maximise this effect, so that the greater the load, the tighter the individual stones in the arch lock together. With perfectly shaped, cut stone, no mortar should be required to keep the arch in place once the central keystone is in position – the shape of the stones and the forces they are subjected to will do this naturally.

For normal-sized openings the best form of curve is a semicircle of the same diameter as the distance between the supporting walls. Measure this accurately; then draw the semicircle on a sheet of firm wood such as blockboard. Roughly saw out the shape; then rasp it down to produce a smoothed arc. This template is now used to cut out a second identical semicircle in the same wood. Unless you are a very skilled woodworker do not attempt to cut out a circle and then saw it in half – slight inaccuracies round the perimeter will not match up, giving the final arch a twisted look.

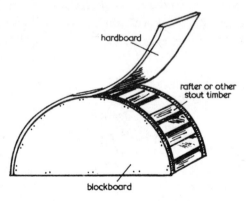

hardboard

rafter or other
stout timber

blockboard

Fig 51 Form for a curved arch

When satisfied with the semicircles, cut lengths of true timber so that each of these, plus the thickness of the blockboard, measure the same as the thickness of the stonework. Use these to assemble the form as shown in Figure 51. A piece of hardboard may now be tacked round the curve and trimmed to size, producing a rigid and exact support and shape for the arch. This is then fixed in position between the stonework supports at the correct height by means of stout timbers, as shown for the double-lintel construction (Fig 47).

The arch stones are built up over the frame from each side as with the peaked arches, and the frame can be marked to indicate the exact centre of the arch to aid positioning of the crowning keystone. Use the stone shapes as illustrated (Fig 50) and avoid great gaps that have to be filled with mortar. If your stone is perfect, the two faces could well extend across the width of the arch – but this is most unlikely. To infill this gap, first allow the outside faces of the arch to harden, and clear away any loose mortar. Select stones that will lock down on to the back of the facing stone, mortar these into position (Fig 52a), or infill with a concrete lintel as described below.

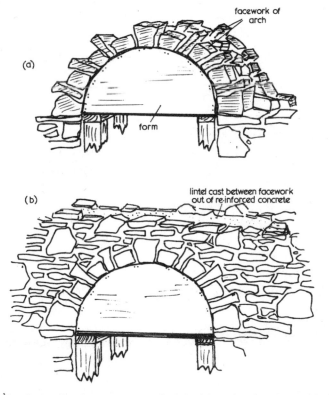

Fig 52 Casting a lintel over a curved arch (a) arch stone in position (b) formation of lintel

Build up the remaining facework over the arch as indicated above, leaving a channel between, except where the faces are tied across. When these are hardened, pour concrete into this channel and lay metal reinforcing rods into the concrete, so that they extend well over the supporting stonework on each side of the archway. When this sets you will have a reinforced concrete lintel *in situ*, bonded to (but invisible) behind the facework (Fig 52b).

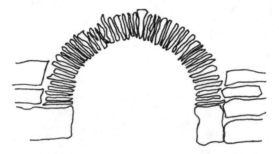

Fig 53 Random arch produced from thin sheets of stone

If shaped stone cannot be obtained, arches may be built on the same principle and by observing the same rules, with very thin sheets of stone (Fig 53) to produce a simple and pleasing effect.

When all is completed, remove the frame and clean up the stonework beneath the arch, even if it means cutting right back and lightly repointing the work. Goggles are essential.

Overhung arches and supports

Apart from the above method of constructing arches where a timber form is required, arches and flared supports can be produced by a technique known as *corbelling* or *overhung building*. A *corbel* is a projection from a wall or some other structure, and by continuously overlapping a series of corbels an arch effect can be produced. Corbelling is particularly effective where a pillar or panel needs to support an overhead structure that does not lie directly above the main support.

Corbelled stonework can only be achieved with a good supply of narrow long stone since most of the length of the stone must be bedded well back over the stone beneath. In other words, the weight of the bulk of the stone counteracts the portion of the stone that is unsupported. For this reason, wide corbelled spans are not recommended, because the stones above the centre of the span, which are subjected to the greatest load, will not be supported by the pillars on each side.

When building a corbelled stone arch, start with the shorter stones first, progressively increasing the length of the stones as the span grows; in this way part of the corbel will always remain over the main stonework support. Small spans are quickly constructed in this manner, which is ideal for producing decorative alcoves in otherwise fairly uniform stone walls, and can be most effective within buildings.

9 Complex Constructions

In this chapter I shall briefly outline a few projects that may be undertaken by the DIY man or woman, concentrating on overall design rather than detailed building procedures.

General Aspects of Design

When considering the building of any complex structure, either within the garden or inside the home, you must give the matter considerable thought long before you hold the trowel in your hand. Stonework is solid and permanent and what you build cannot be folded up and tucked away when not in use, like a deck chair after summer is over. The following points may prevent you from building your personal folly.

Do avoid considering your project in isolation from the rest of the environment in which it is to be carried out. With a new property or unplanned garden you may be able to build round this major project; otherwise, it will have to fit in with existing features. Try to match your materials and your style to those already there. If what is in existence is offensive, tear the lot down and start from scratch. Work to link together all features of your environment, instead of chopping it up into separate little areas. This means making the house and garden come together as well.

Functional Garden Projects

Barbecues
In the UK the majority of people consider a garden barbecue either a decadent luxury, a rich man's toy, or a means of impressing the neighbours. In the US the barbecue is regarded as a sensible and enjoyable normal part of life, capturing many of the delights of a picnic without the inconvenience. It is

unfortunate that the barbecue is not given a more important role in Britain: it has unique advantages. Young children delight in eating out of doors, unrestrained by the formalities of eating at the table – their conservatism in taste disappears. Simple meals for the housewife become exciting, while the barbecue seems to bring out the latent master *chef* in the most kitchen-shy of husbands. Teenagers can be left to their own devices, to 'do their own thing', happily, without disturbing the rest of the home. For the socially minded wife a barbecue party offers welcome relief from cookery books, the best tableware, and having to don that smart, but uncomfortable, dress. Outdoor parties can and should be given on the spur of the moment – little preparation needs to be done and the washing-up afterwards is considerably reduced.

The main argument against the use of a barbecue in the UK is the unpredictability of our weather, but many a wet sunrise becomes a brilliant summer sunset. Build your barbecue and enjoy the flexibility it provides – instead of applying the same rules to it as you do to the ordered routine of your kitchen.

Siting the barbecue

A barbecue can be as simple as a metal mesh supported over a fire by a few bricks or as complex as that of the integrated barbecue area in Plate 9. The choice is yours, but in terms of permanent natural stonework features, it is with the latter type of barbecue area that we are concerned. The barbecue area must not be too far from the house and kitchen, so that it is easier to work between the two – especially when it comes to washing up. Do not plan the barbecue in the bottom of a dip – the cook will not want to stand in a puddle all evening. Lay an underground electricity supply to the area before you start building – the fun often starts as the light fades. Avoid building the barbecue against the house – smoke blackens most materials in time. Try to site the barbecue area where it will look good in the overall design of the garden, not forgetting that it will be used almost exclusively in the afternoon and evening when the sun will be in the West. Try and provide a little shelter from wind for the actual cooking area.

Notes on construction

The barbecue itself (Plate 10) will incorporate a number of building features that have already been discussed, but these will occur very close together instead of allowing you long runs of straight walling. Draw up a well-annotated plan before you start, so that you do not miss anything essential as you build. The barbecue itself has three basic functional components; the hearth for the fire, a metal framework over the fire to support pans or food; and a work top on which to place food when it is not being cooked. The addition of other features, such as ovens and fuel stores, are not essential but can be incorporated as you wish.

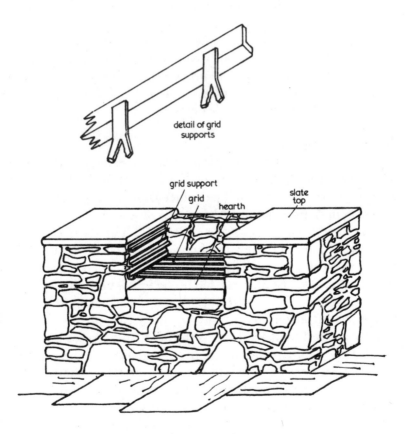

Fig 54 Basic form of stone barbecue

I have generally built barbecues with the cheapest and oldest form of fuel in mind, namely wood. You can, if you wish, burn charcoal, or even set a gas burner on the hearth. But you cannot burn anything but gas or charcoal on a barbecue specifically designed to burn gas or charcoal – and gas and charcoal are expensive. Providing a wood fire (not huge logs) takes a little practice, and the metal grid must be capable of being raised or lowered so that it remains in close contact with the fire. This is achieved by setting angled supports at different heights above the hearth on which the grid rests. Start with plenty of wood, heating it all up; then lower the grid to do the cooking over the fiercely glowing, but no longer smoking, wood embers (Fig 54).

The hearth itself can simply be a thick slab of paving stone. This will undoubtedly crack and become pitted in time but that is not really important. It is far simpler to construct, and produces a much better reflected heat than undertaking the complicated task of building-in a separate fire basket.

The working tops – one on each side – should be of a single piece of smooth stone. Once again, polished slate is ideal if you can obtain it. These can be kept clean with the wipe of a cloth and withstand the hottest of pans. Keep all your working surfaces at a comfortable height, including the grill. Also, pave the area of ground immediately round the barbecue so that the *chef* has a firm, clean, dry area on which to stand. Keep the basic design of the cooking area simple and add other features as you require them, such as a stone seat and woodshed. Do not attempt to build so much into the barbecue that it begins to resemble your kitchen!

Children's play areas

It may seem strange at first sight to mention the subject of children's play areas in the garden in a book on natural stonework. But to give them thought at the outset is important on two counts. A play area totally belonging to young children means that they are less likely to disturb the rest of the garden but, more important, their play area can be transformed into a garden feature once they grow up. Thus consider this part of the garden, too, in terms of future use as a part of the whole area. Do not divide off a rectangular area if your garden is based upon loops, curves, and circles. Remember that the infant's sandpit can later become a garden pool, and shape it imaginatively.

Fuel stores

Many an attractively laid-out garden is marred by the presence of concrete coal-bunkers and fuel tanks. Using natural random stone, the appearance of these may either be hidden or improved, and such an exercise is perhaps the best way for the DIY man to introduce himself to the problems of complex constructions in stone.

Domestic fuel tanks are invariably of the gravity-feed type and are thus placed in a raised and conspicuous position close to the house. Hiding them is difficult but not impossible, providing their siting is not completely wrong. Enclosing them in a solid high wall should not be attempted, because this only draws attention to their presence. A more effective method is to use a combination of walling and pilasters or pillars with light trellis-work between (Plate 6).

Quick-climbing, densely leafing plants, such as honeysuckle and clematis, planted at the base of the pillars can be trained over the trellis, not only softening or hiding the tank but also providing an attractive and colourful backdrop in its own right. The top of the wall can also be left open, so that climbers and trailing plants (particularly nasturtiums, which thrive in poor soils) can fall down over the face of the wall, giving even better cover.

Coal-bunkers can be approached in two ways. If you have a garden on different levels, they can be sunk into the ground; if not, at least they can be built out of stone to match the rest of the stonework in the garden. If the bunker is deep it need not be wide – half a ton of loose coal takes up less than 1m x 1m x 1m in volume – so an excavator is not necessary to dig the ground away. If possible, site the bunker behind a retaining wall, and build the wall leaving a gap as for steps. Dig out and line the bunker with old brick or concrete block, and concrete the floor so that it slopes gently from back and sides to the access opening in front. This will not only drain the bunker, should water seep into it, but will also help to move the coal to the opening. Face off by finishing the retaining wall across the front of the bunker, leaving an access hole at the base large enough to accommodate a shovel with ease. A long slab of stone can be used as a lintel across this opening. Lay slabs over the top of the bunker supported on lintels, or cast a reinforced-concrete slab on a wooden frame to fit, paving on top with random stone. But remember to leave an opening for deliveries. The provision of a large removable slab is the simplest solution for this.

Raised solid-fuel stores are best built against an outbuilding or existing wall. These should be 'lean-to' shaped – single-sided roof – like purchased bunkers and built of block faced with stone. Make the top of stout timber so that the whole lid lifts up – this is better than leaving just an access hole. It makes cleaning out once in a while much easier and will allow the bunker to be used for either wood or coal (or both, if a partition is made).

Outbuildings

It is beyond the scope of this book to provide a DIY guide to building a house extension out of natural stone. However, having experimented with stone and by using this book, together with more conventional building manuals, the enterprising DIY person might be tempted to try out acquired skills by designing and constructing an outbuilding. At least, mistakes are less important here and valuable experience can be gained.

In this context, however, I shall restrict the term 'outbuilding' to small garden sheds or greenhouses – not a set of stables or a barn! The building laws and principles remain the same as for brick or block work, and putting in the foundations and floor proceeds in the same way, except that the foundations should be stronger and wider than normal to accommodate the heavier and bulkier stone. Cavity work is not essential in an outbuilding, so the stonework is built against, and tied into, an internal skin of blocks. A polythene membrane sandwiched between the two will give quite adequate damp-proofing. A damp-proof course should also be incorporated just above ground-level right round the building. Precast-concrete lintels can be used over the windows and doors on the blockwork, and if the wall plate that supports the rafters is placed on this level, the falling pitch of the roof will remove the complication of constructing lintels over the stonework (Chapter 10). Remember to build the blockwork and stonework together, and tie the stone to the block. Details of setting in door and window frames are discussed in the following chapter.

The natural stone-and-timber glasshouse is a less expensive – and far more attractive – DIY proposition than buying a 'kit', particularly if the stoneworker has had woodworking experience as well. Here damp-proofing is unnecessary and the stonework simply consists of an exterior enclosed rectangle of walling with an internal face of block. An opening is left for the door at one end of the rectangle, and the timberwork to support the glass is built on to the course of blocks to suit you. With all buildings, remember to put in good concrete foundations and to level off below ground before you start building.

The Integrated Terrace

The most pleasing way of linking the house to the garden is by means of what I have termed an *integrated terrace*, which is part of both house and garden. Functionally and aesthetically it is an extension of both environments and can greatly increase the use and enjoyment of your garden. The integrated terrace, however, is *not* an area of paving slabs outside the kitchen or lounge, but fits into the overall structure of the home. Enclosing such a terrace by a low wall improves the appearance of the area belonging to the house without totally isolating it from the garden. However, if you try this, remember to drain the terrace through the walls.

The type of terrace illustrated in Plate 11 makes use of most of the separate building techniques and structures discussed already, but walling, paving, pillars, and steps are all combined in one integrated whole. Such a structure is well within the scope of the DIY person who has mastered the basic principles.

This particular terrace shows some very good and carefully thought-out design features apart from its overall addition to both house and garden. There are several points of access – not merely one – from both house and garden. The steps are off-centred and provide a pleasing curved contrast to the general regularity of design, which is further broken by varying the height dimension with wall panel and pillars. The pergola can also be placed in an attractive position, not extending over the whole terrace but supported on pillars part-way, allowing variable areas of full sunlight and shade. A small room extension in stone balances the whole design.

Too often so little thought is given to terrace design that it spoils both house and garden instead of enhancing them. Be bold when considering such a structure: avoid simply thinking of tacking it on to part of the house – be prepared to wrap it around a corner and vary heights. Over-emphasis on plans tends to suppress the ability to think in three-dimensional terms. Plans are important but a three-dimensional approach is essential for good design.

Functional Areas in the Home

Fireplaces
The most common feature built out of stone within the home is the fireplace, which may be constructed of stone even where the building itself is made from artificial materials. Most people enjoy an open fire and yet, for the sake of convenience, they opt for central heating. This 'convenience', however, is becoming more and more expensive, and in the future the presence of oil-fired central heating, in particular, may be a disadvantage, rather than an asset, when selling a house. What is not often appreciated is that a combination of the two can be not only comfortable but comforting, and the little extra effort well worthwhile.

Open fires are seen at their best in bold natural surroundings, and the stone fireplace is irreplaceable in this respect (Plate 12). For those lucky enough to own an old stone cottage, the original fireplace is probably still there but covered over. To resurrect it is a simple matter of renovation – and possibly slight alteration to suit personal taste – and is discussed in the next chapter. For the person with a more modern home and fireplace, on the other hand, it will be a matter rather of building from scratch, and certain aspects of design will be all-important.

The fireplace, hearth, and so on can either be built wholly out of stone, or out of brick cladded with stone. Whichever method is chosen, remember that the total structure must not be small; it must be big and bold and the focal point of the room. Stone fireplaces cannot be built in tiny rooms and, ideally, they should be an integral part of the whole wall. Keep their continuity by creating stone alcoves, ledges, and the like for stereo, books, logs, and the television set.

A mantelpiece is not an essential part of a fireplace. A bold unbroken sweep of beautifully fitted stonework can be far more pleasing than an ugly projection cluttered with odds and ends. The fireplace and chimney breast can be built in a curve to produce a concave effect that adds its own particular charm.

In spite of appearances there is no law that demands that the hearth itself should be at floor-level. Having experimented a little, I have decided I get most pleasure from a fire that burns some 25–30cm (about 1ft) above the ground. Not only does it warm most of my bulk when in an armchair beside it, but the hearth is exactly the right height for my feet!

It may be prudent to avoid wooden lintels when building a new fireplace since these are something of a fire risk. They are, however, most attractive in old buildings and, if replaced again, they can be well chamfered at the back to reduce the amount of timber overhanging the fire. Otherwise, use a strong stone lintel or cast a lintel *in situ* on a frame faced with stone as described in Chapters 8 and 10.

Make the grate area large so that it will accommodate those bulky chunks of wood nobody seems to want because they will not split easily. Use a firebrick back and sides to prevent the stone from splitting and cracking in the heat, and make sure the chimney is throated or you may have problems with smoke billowing into the room. With this in mind, it also helps if you don't set the lintel back too far over the hearth or too high above it. Finally, buy a good dog grate and burn your fuel on that. It is a good idea to leave the final height of the hearth until last so that you can judge its best position by burning a few fires on the grate, propped up by bricks to different levels.

To prevent smoke seepage, ensure that all joints between stones are well-mortared and be prepared to repoint any areas of mortar shrinkage after the fire has been well used. A little smoke the first couple of days after building is nothing to worry about; wait until the chimney gets warmed up properly to see how it normally behaves.

Floors

Concrete bases covered with mortar screeds that can be carpeted or tiled have largely replaced natural stone floors since they are generally easier to clean and more comfortable to walk on. Cut stone 'tiles', however, can still be used with modern basic construction techniques; and with polished slates and marbles, beautiful, smooth (though expensive) finishes can be obtained. A concrete base incorporating a damp proof membrane is laid first and levelled off as accurately as possible. A perfect level can then be produced on this surface with a self levelling floor compound (of a type to which mortar can be bonded).

The actual tiling is by means of a horizontal cladding, rather than a paving, technique since the stone serves a decorative – not a structural – function. The stones are laid in a mortar bed to which a bonder has been added and the backs of the stone can also be painted with bonder to increase adhesion. The stones must be flush with each other, not only for appearance and comfort but also to prevent accidents. Also remember to allow for easy clearance by doors when working out final floor heights. Unlike paving, grouting is done after the stonework has set and a wet mix, almost a slurry (consistency 4–5), is used. This is spread over the floor and worked well into the joints. Then *immediately* (the grout must still be wet) fine sawdust is brushed over the surface of the floor. This absorbs the water and particles from the surface of the stones so cleaning them. A first application is followed by a second one of more clean sawdust which removes all traces of the wet grout from the stone.

If the flooring is a little uneven or a more polished finish is required, laid floors can be ground down with a mechanical floor grinder. These are obtainable from certain hire firms but require some practice to use well and are also messy. Because of the great problems involved, do not attempt to build stone or concrete floors above ground-floor level.

Other structures

In larger houses, room may be available to use stone wall panels as features or to build in stone cocktail bars and so on. Since these are really integral parts of the building and probably of little interest to the amateur they need not be discussed here. Other features are examined in the next chapter under the general heading of Renovation.

10 Demolition and Renovation

Much of the work described so far has concerned the use of stone in the garden. This chapter is devoted solely to the house and is written largely for those people who own, or are contemplating buying, a stone cottage. I will concentrate on the restoration and improvement of the original structure and set aside the greater problems, such as adding extensions. For those of you already committed to an extension I will make the observation that nowadays these are largely grant-aided and, as such, often involve the addition to an old property of bathroom and lavatory built out of modern materials. The only part of a renovated cottage I was staying in that froze up with the associated havoc of burst pipes was the grant-aided extension!

If you have just purchased an old property in need of renovation, the first rule is not to rush into making alterations immediately. If at all possible, live in the place, camp in it in the summer if it *is* in a poor condition, and try to learn a little of its history, gain some of its atmosphere, and see how it reacts to changes in the weather. In this way you may discover, before it's too late, why picture windows are not a good idea on one side of the house, and where the leaks are, *before* you decorate.

Do not attempt to live inside the house once you start making structural alterations, however much fun it may seem at the start. Building work, especially internal work, nearly always takes longer than the most pessimistic of estimates and, whereas a single person might just cope with the inevitable squalor and inconvenience, marriages rapidly become strained. If necessary, put a caravan in the garden and live in that; the harmony and increased efficiency in working unhampered by domestic routine and clutter will more than make up for the additional initial cost.

I have to admit that I myself made a mess of renovating and modernising my own old cottage many years ago. This was due to a combination of ignoring the above guidelines, wishing to get the work finished quickly, using modern materials too exclusively and changing the character of the cottage; with the help of builders, I turned a home into a house. My only consolation is that it made me take a far more personal interest in my efforts for other people, and the lesson taught me to be a far wiser user of stone.

Although I am going to treat demolition and renovation in separate sections, this is purely for descriptive convenience. The two processes should operate together, and the person who reduces an old cottage to its basic shell before starting to rebuild must have profit alone in mind.

Demolition

The best way to gain some knowledge of how old cottages are built is to study a few ruins carefully. This will not only give you some insight into the basic original layout of your home, but also highlights the structural strong points of the whole dwelling. Modern building methods differ in many ways from the traditional ones, and observation of the remains of a basic 'two-up, two-down' old stone cottage will immediately reveal useful information. Most important, it will show that the original pine ends of the cottage are the main support structures for the whole building – and are often all that remains in very old buildings. The roof is entirely supported by the pine end, unlike modern buildings where the pine end may be built to the roof. The roof construction itself also differs, the main weight generally being carried by massive *purlins*, except in very old buildings where the *cruck beams* or curved timber roof-supports, are all-important. Fireplaces are invariably present together with unlined chimneys in both pine ends, although they need not necessarily be centrally placed.

The walls will taper from the ground to the eaves, the batter generally being most pronounced on the internal side of the walls: differences in thickness of up to 25cm (10in) are not uncommon. The stonework itself will have no central cavity; instead, the two faces will be infilled with a mixture of lime-mortar and smaller rubble. Where a horizontal level is required, a strip of timber is often inserted into the stonework. You should also notice that the most massive stones occur in the bottom of the walling, smaller stones generally being used towards the roof. Modern-type foundations will be completely absent; instead, you may find that the cottage is sited on the natural foundation of a bed-rock outcrop that may even form part of the lower wall.

With such information in mind, examine your own property critically and see how it compares. The cottage you own may have been altered already, though many years ago, since it was built. Be particularly wary of 'roomy' cottages – what you may mistake for an internal partition wall could well be an original pine end on to which an extension has been added and well matched. Look for signs of a fireplace – these are usually sited in the pine ends. If there is one, then restrain yourself from knocking out this wall to make a nice big sitting-room in the centre of the house: you are more likely to end up with a nice big pile of building stone in the centre of a building plot! Get to know your propety well before you even start *planning* to demolish anything.

Houses are built from the ground upwards and, ideally, demolition should proceed in the reverse order. However, this is rarely practical, so a compromise approach must be adopted, bearing in mind a golden rule of demolition. Whatever you knock down is supporting something above it which will also fall. Demolition experts razing whole buildings to the ground seek to remove the minimum number of key supports to produce the maximum effect. So take care! If you wish to knock out stonework to make an opening for a window or door, make sure you know exactly what is both above and around the proposed opening. Many old buildings have been plastered over so that the structural work, and thus the possible hazards, are hidden.

A stubborn old friend recounted how he had built a bathroom extension on his cottage before putting in the doorway. Unfortunately, just where he proposed to insert the doorway a chunk of quoin stone that weighed almost a quarter of a ton projected no more than a few inches into the selected area. Had he stripped off the plaster before he started he would not have had the problem of re-siting the opening. In many old properties the plasterwork has degenerated through dampness and time, and in the long run its removal will be less bothersome than continuously patching it up. Hack it off, and this will show you not only the character of the stonework but also reveal the true state of any electrical wiring. Re-render and plaster the whole room, if you wish, when the structural alterations are complete.

Demolition invariably produces mountains of material but do not simply look upon it as waste and barrow it lock, stock, and barrel into a skip. Certain items *are* best disposed of – I've yet to find a use for hacked-off plaster, which is even poor filling material. Tin sheeting, old wiring, and rotten lino can also be discarded, but look carefully at the supposedly rotten timbers you take out. The damage may be confined to the ends where they were embedded in the wall, and worm-holes may be only superficial, so that the timber may be quite usable elsewhere. Besides, the fireplace you are going to restore is going to devour wood uncritically so, at the very least, you are throwing away free fuel!

The old slates or tiles on the building may have to be replaced if you are considering an extension, because the roof should match throughout. Remove them carefully. Just as you found it extremely difficult to get matching slates for your new roof and have had to resort to tiles, somebody else is experiencing the same problem. The old slates are worth money and can offset the cost of the new tiles. Slates can be used over and over again, and many a modern extension bears the same roof that once, long ago, kept the rain off farm animals.

The greatest demolition treasure for the DIY stoneworker, however, is the actual building stone, and this for two main reasons. Firstly, it is the perfect match for doing any new building on the property and, secondly, because it has been used for building before you therefore know it can be used again – in no way is it rubble to be discarded! Similarly, the flagstones on the kitchen floor, the old slate working tops in the pantry, and any solid stone steps are all items that may be used again, either in the house or garden, but which would cost a fortune to reproduce out of virgin rock. Sort and store all these materials for future re-use. In that way, although you may alter the shape, and perhaps a little of the character of your cottage, you will help to maintain its integrity.

The main tools of demolition are the bar, pick, lump hammer and cold chisel – not the sledgehammer as most people seem to think. You want to preserve the materials, not smash them into useless fragments. Demolition can be as slow as construction *and* as frustrating at times. Stone should be removed piece by piece as far as possible, then cleaned, sorted, and stored in various piles (*See* Chapter 2). The hardest stone to get out will usually be the first one, and particularly so in well matched and tied stonework. Look critically over the whole structure and select a stone that not only looks as though it may come out without too much trouble but will also allow easy access to the neighbouring stones. Clear away mortar and chinking-stone from around it and then work the stone loose by cutting deeply, and levering from side to side and up and down.

If making an opening for a window or door make the hole considerably larger than you require, this is extremely important to allow you room in which to work to tie-in the new returns to the existing stonework. All the time you work upwards, take away the stone in an arch so that the stonework remains self-supporting (Fig 55). Should you try to cut out the stone in a rectangular manner, the stone overhead will fall on you. When removing an old lintel or beam, do not attempt to pull the lintel away and see what happens. Cut the stone out in a rough self-supporting (if fragile) arch-shape above the lintel, and *then* remove it – otherwise, it is likely that a whole section of walling may fall.

Whenever making any sort of opening, first check to see which way the joists and rafters run. These will almost always be at right angles to the pine ends; thus the side wall of the house will be supporting the upstairs floors. It is essential that

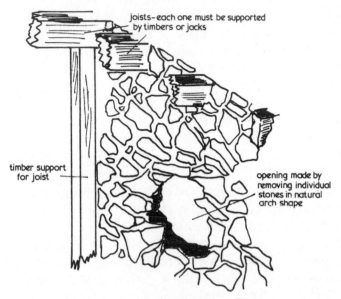

Fig 55 Making an opening in an old wall

any beam that is going to lie above the proposed opening be firmly supported before the opening is made. It can be supported either by means of a jack (*See* Chapter 1) or by a stout piece of timber, but remember to leave sufficient working space between it and the wall.

If you discover the fireplace but wish to alter its design, do not knock the chimney breast around more than absolutely necessary. It is far simpler to build over it and still use the original chimney, than to have to shape and seal the inside of a new one.

Where repointing work is to be done, cut away the old lime mortar as deeply as possible and also remove loose pieces of chinking and packing stone.

Avoid taking risks with either yourself or the building during demolition work – think of the consequences before you start. Do not leave unsupported stonework at the end of the day; the trespasser may well be *your own child*! If you have safety equipment, use it – if you do not, buy it.

Renovation

Actual rebuilding techniques are exactly those already described the only difference being that you will be building to existing structures rather than starting afresh. The cardinal rule is to ensure that your new work is tied well into the existing structure, particularly at corners where the temptation not to bother is the greatest. Here, existing quoin stone must be removed at intervals, and your work carried into these cavities. Similarly, partition walls meeting existing walls at right angles must be tied-in at intervals (Fig 56).

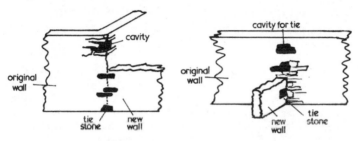

Fig 56 Tying new walls into original walls

Walls

One of the most important of improvement jobs is damp proofing the walls; this should be carried out by a reliable firm giving a long-term guarantee. Generally, it is achieved by inserting a copper strip in the stonework just above ground-level. Unfortunately, it seems that such firms fail to give their employees any training in stonework: the strip is held in place with mortar, but this is usually done with a wet mix slapped and smeared all over the surrounding stonework, apparently with a shovel! From the outset, make it clear that every joint is to be pointed the way you want it – you're going to be paying enough, after all – and it is then up to you whether or not to plaster over the work in the end: the choice is yours, as it should be.

Adopt the same approach with electrical wiring. If you've

cleaned out the old lime-mortar joints deeply, ask the electrician to follow the line of the joints and to pin his cable between the stones. Switches and power points can be built in by removing a large stone, setting the holding-box in place, then building it in with smaller stone. Leave the actual repointing, like plastering, to the very end. Use a dryish but plastic and malleable mix and add a bonder if you wish to. Fill the joints well but neatly. Then, when the mix begins to go off, cut back and point-up to the style you want with the cutting-out knife, being sure that you do not disturb the joints (*See* Chapter 3). Some people prefer to paint over the stonework finally with a clear polyurethane preparation that cuts down dust and produces a certain amount of shine. Personally, I don't like this but am not prepared to argue strongly.

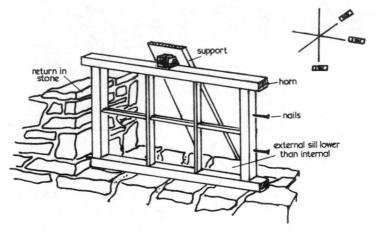

Fig 57 Building in a new window frame

Doors and window frames

How to make the openings has already been described and need not be repeated. Since there is no cavity, the frames should be positioned well back in the wall to provide some protection against the weather. The frames may also have a strip of damp-proof course material tacked round them to reduce the movement of any moisture from the walls into the wood. Build up the inside of the wall to a position level with the bottom of the frame, making sure that it is perfectly level. The outside walling should be levelled off several centimetres lower in order to accommodate a sill and provide a fall to shed water away from the frame.

Bang a couple of large nails firmly (but only partway) into the outside of the upright arms of the frame, and set the frame on a good bed of mortar towards the inside wall. Ensure that the frame is the correct way round and is both horizontal and upright. Use props to hold it rigidly in place, and then start building the returns progressively on each side and on both inside and outside faces (Fig 57). The stonework should either fit snugly to the frame or slightly overlap it. Join-up tightly to the frame with mortar and lock the nails on to a tie-stone between the inner and outer wall faces. Infill tightly with stone and mortar between the faces and build up the sides until they are just fractionally lower than the top of the frame. Allow to set hard before attempting to put the lintel in place.

Lintels

A lintel is basically a supporting structure spanning a gap below and carrying a load above. Thus the arches described previously (*See* Chapter 8) can be regarded as lintels, but here we shall deal only with horizontal lintels over windows, doors, and so on. Such lintels fall into two main categories: those that are pre-formed and lifted complete into place, and those that are built *in situ*.

There are many types of pre-formed lintel, and perhaps the simplest and cheapest is the reinforced-concrete lintel that can be purchased in a variety of sizes. It is used wherever the work is to be rendered over, but cannot be exposed in faced stonework where it looks totally out of place. Thus, in renovation work a lintel of this kind will mainly be confined to internal walls that are to be plastered over and to any external building that will subsequently be rendered over. If used as a last resort on facework, it should either be cladded or covered over with timber, but this is not so satisfactory.

Specially shaped metal lintels marketed under the name

'Catnic' have been produced for facework and expose only a very thin metal edge to the surface. Details of these can be obtained from most builders' suppliers.

Wooden lintels are extremely effective and very much in character with old buildings (*See* Plate 4), but they should be of a seasoned long-lasting hardwood, such as oak, and will be difficult and expensive to obtain new. Before fitting, they must be well protected with a proofing chemical. Sound portions of old structural beams obtained during demolition and also old wooden railway sleepers make excellent wooden lintels.

The best pre-formed lintel is a single slab of cut stone, long enough to comfortably span the gap, and both thick enough and deep enough to support the weight of stonework above. These will have to be obtained either as reclaimed lintels from old demolition sites or cut especially for you. Failing this, old window-sills and solid steps can provide shortish lintels for smaller windows.

In the case of lintels that are cast *in situ*, two approaches are possible. Either they can be cast on a thin, well supported sheet of stone, such as slate, which is left in place after the supporting timbers are removed, or they can be built on a timber frame – like the arch technique – that is subsequently removed. For both appearance and strength, the latter type of lintel should always be slightly arched and have a central keystone.

Pre-formed lintels are bedded on to a good depth of mortar on the returns on each side of the frame, and a layer of mortar trowelled along the top of the frame is gently squeezed out to provide a good seal. No weight should be supported by the frame or it will become distorted. It is a good precaution to provide a firm prop beneath the frame until the stonework has hardened. Do not lay a line of evenly matched stones over the top of the lintel, but maintain the pattern of building you have adopted with the rest of the stonework, and be sure to tie the ends of the lintel well in.

For the lintel cast *in situ* on a thin stone sheet, set the sheet on the returns, as with a pre-formed lintel, and ensure that it is both horizontal and well supported beneath. Carry the internal and external facework over and above the sheet but leave the cavity between unfilled. Allow the stonework to set; then cast your own concrete lintel, reinforced with an iron rod, in one action into this cavity. When all has hardened, the supports can be removed. To build a separate stone lintel, build the necessary frame and, with selected shaped stone, construct the lintel facing on the framework as described for arches (*See* Chapter 8). Again, cast your own concrete lintel between the facework and remove the frame when all is well set.

Sills

The best window-sills are produced from single pieces of stone cut to size and in character with the rest of the work. Ideally, sills should be inserted beneath the window frame before the external returns are started and then the latter built on to the sill. Unfortunately, sills are very often regarded purely as a 'finish' and something to adorn with window boxes. Lovely as these can be, a sill should primarily prevent water seeping back into the wall by overlipping it by at least 3cm (1in), grooving it underneath the lip and sloping it downwards and outwards. Once again, try and get hold of some slate, as it is probably the best natural material for the sill.

Indoor arches

For arches within the home – a picturesque alternative to doorways – proceed as described for garden arches. However, remember to ensure that there is sufficient headroom for the arch, leaving enough space above for the reinforced internal lintel to carry the weight of floor or wall. Such arches are a strong and safe method of allowing access through a pine-end supporting wall. Arched alcoves can also be used to offset a large expanse of internal stone wall. These are most easily built on the corbel principle described in Chapter 8.

Ceilings and floors

Building regulations often require that rooms be of a minimum height to qualify for grants. This can be achieved either by raising a ceiling or by lowering the floor. Downstairs, the latter is generally the easier, but watch out for two things.

Beneath that thin concrete skim or flagstone floor you might encounter solid bedrock. There is also a danger that if you lower the floor you will get flooded out every time it rains. What at first sight may appear the obvious thing to do, with hindsight may not have been the best approach.

Pantries

If your cottage has a stone-built pantry don't just knock it down to make a bigger kitchen – extend your kitchen in another direction. A good stone-built pantry will do almost all that your fridge can and more. Furthermore, the slate or marble working top that is probably already installed is, I'm assured by my wife, unbeatable for producing good pastry.

Fireplaces

Fireplaces have already been discussed in Chapter 9 and here I will confine myself to the renovation of the original stone fireplace in your cottage. Firstly, you can be certain that there is a fireplace there somewhere, even if it's been bricked-up and plastered-over. There will often be more than one. If you cannot find it, go outside and look for the position of the stacks. If there aren't any, and the place has already had some alterations carried out on it, get up on to the roof and determine where the stacks have been taken down and roofed-over.

When you have discovered where the fireplaces are sited – and these will only be on the ground floor in old country cottages – start stripping away the plaster on the appropriate wall. Keep a look-out for brickwork in the stone, or for a straight vertical joint indicating a sealed opening. Expose the opening and remove the debris; then clean down the whole of the wall. Many old fireplaces were gradually bricked-up, first to accommodate an open range, then perhaps a smaller coal fire, before being blocked off completely. Go back to the original and decide whether or not you like it.

Often these old fireplaces were massive open hearths and a solid beam acted as the supporting lintel. If this has been covered over it is probably not very sound and must be replaced. Remember the advice on demolition! You may not, however, require such a massive opening – so the removal of the old beam will give you a chance to reduce the opening, while at the same time altering the design to your personal requirements.

Before attempting to light the fire, do be sure to sweep the chimney and to examine and repair the stack (*and* the chimney-pot), if necessary.

External cleaning

Good exterior stonework should never be painted or rendered: the beauty is in the stone. Such precautions were adopted years ago mainly to weather-proof the lime-mortar joints. With modern cement mortars and additives this is unnecessary, and old limewash and render can be hacked away, wire-brushed, and hosed down to remove all traces of them, and the cleaned stonework be repointed. This also helps to match the extension to the original. When whitewash and the like are difficult to remove, employ a firm that specialises in sand-blasting – it will be well worth the expense.

This short chapter hardly does justice to the vast amount of knowledge and experience needed to deal with major renovation and building work. It is merely intended as a guide, to give you confidence to embark on some of the minor projects yourselves, and also to give you a wider understanding of what can be achieved, which may be useful whether it is you or a builder who undertakes the work. Neither attempt more than you are confident you can achieve, nor accept less than you are led to expect, or hope for, from a proclaimed 'expert'.

Conclusion

The intention of this book has been to both guide and stimulate the reader rather than to provide a total A–Z manual on stonework. Much deserves to be expanded on, even more remains to be said, but if the basic information has aroused interest, provided you with enough confidence to make a start, and saves you money, the book will have achieved its main objectives. Whether or not you intend to build with stone yourself, I hope I have provided you with a greater appreciation of the work that exists all around you. Perhaps now you will not walk past an old wall without noticing it. Study both old and modern stonework with a newly critical eye – it can teach you more than can words alone. If you are designing your own home extension or garden, but intend to have the work carried out by contractors, I hope I have given you a greater understanding of what is possible, together with some of the problems involved. I hope you will be able to appreciate natural stonework in terms of a balanced expression in thought, labour, craftsmanship, and artistry.

For the DIY stoneworker or the professional intending to work in stone, I wish to add a few final words of warning. No book is a substitute for experience, and creative, if not perceptive, experience requires time to develop. Having read this book, you may know something about stonework. Until you've tried, you know nothing about working with stone. Always start from the beginning; if possible labour for someone who *does* work with stone for a while, and master every task however basic or menial. If you cannot make a good mix you will be unable to build good random-stone walls – if you can, show somebody else how to mix and devote all *your* spare time to building.

Try not to be lazy and settle for less than the best. Be critical of your own work and think out how you would change it if you did the job over again. In this way, with every new job you approach you will consciously strive to do better than last time and will often succeed. In the light of experience I am no longer satisfied with some of the early stonework I carried out, but I still feel proud of it because it was my best at the time and I learned what present skills I have from doing it.

As you become more skilled you will begin to develop your own style of building, and not only craftmanship but also artistry will begin to show. The work will be recognisable as *yours* and no other person's; so you must be sure that it is your best at the time. Be proud of what you do and make it worth preserving. Should someone some day wish to knock it down, build it well so that it doesn't collapse with the first blow from a sledgehammer. Not only make them work when they take down your wall – make them also doubt whether or not they can build better!

Random-natural stonework is perhaps the most demanding of all building work, but it is also the most rewarding. Your stonework is your monument but, unlike many other monuments, it should be both beautiful and useful too.

APPENDIX

TABLE 1

Area/Weight Relationship for Average Limestones of Various Shapes and Sizes

(Denser stone, such as slate, will give approximately a 10–20% reduction in area per unit weight of stone.)

Type of stone	Shape of stone	Approx. area built per tonne (ton) m^2	sq yd
Walling*	Rectangular thin stones laid flat	2.2	2.6
	Randomised stone of all shapes	2.5	3.0
	Regular uniform blocks of stone	3.0	3.6
Paving	5–10cm thick (2–4in)	7.5–8	9–10
	5cm thick (2in)	10	12
	3–5cm thick (1–2in)	14–16	17–19
	2–4cm thick ($\frac{3}{4}$–$1\frac{1}{2}$in)	17.5–20	21–24
Cladding	1cm thick ($\frac{3}{8}$in)	40–45	48–54

* This table refers to single face only – quantities must be doubled for free-standing walls with two faces.

TABLE 2

Various Types of Mixes for
Different Construction Projects in Stone

Type of mix	Type of work	Sand–Cement Ratio	Consistency*	Additives
	Infilling	8–10 : 1	2–3	
	Foundations	6–8 : 1	4–5	all in aggregate
Concretes	Bases	6–8 : 1	4–5	
	Lintels	4–6 : 1	4	
	General walling	5–7 : 1	1–2	Plasticiser
	Topping-off	4–5 : 1	2–3	Plasticiser and bonder
	Coping	4 : 1	2–3	Plasticiser and bonder
	Pointing (internal)	3–4 : 1	1–2	Plasticiser
Mortars	Pointing (external)	3–4 : 1	1–2	Waterproofer
	Paving (thick)	6–8 : 1	2–3	None
	Paving (thin)	4–6 : 1	3–4	None
	Grouting	2–3 : 1	0	None
	Cladding	3 : 1	3	Bonder
	Flooring (tiles)	4–6 : 1	3–4	Bonder
	Fireplaces	Special fixative for hearth and firebricks		
Special	Barbecues			
	Pools (lining)	1 : 2–4	5 (slurry)	Waterproofer

* Wetness scale from 0–5, equivalent to no water (0) up to a very wet mix (5).

TABLE 3

Some Additives Available for Use in Stonework Mortars

Type of additive	Product name		
	(FEB LTD)	(UNIBOND LTD)	(SEALOCRETE PRODUCTS LTD)
Plasticiser	Febmix* Admix	Uniplas	Plaz
Waterproofer	Febproof*	—	Sealopruf
Bonder	Febbond PVA	Unibond*	Sealobond
Hardener	Febspeed*	—	Sealoset
Frost-Proofer			Sealofrost
Colorant	Febtone	—	Sealantone
Cladding Bonder	Febtile	Unibond	Sealotak
Masonary Cleaner	—	Wipe	Sealoclean

* Personal preference

Index